Listen, Sister!

Listen, Sister!

FINDING HOPE IN THE FREAKSHOW OF LIFE

Tess Scott

NASHVILLE

NEW YORK • LONDON • MELBOURNE • VANCOUVER

Listen, Sister!

Finding Hope in the Freakshow of Life

Published in New York, New York, by Morgan James Publishing. Morgan James is a trademark of Morgan James, LLC. www.MorganJamesPublishing.com

Proudly distributed by Ingram Publisher Services.

Morgan James BOGO™

A **FREE** ebook edition is available for you or a friend with the purchase of this print book.

_____

CLEARLY SIGN YOUR NAME ABOVE

Instructions to claim your free ebook edition:
1. Visit MorganJamesBOGO.com
2. Sign your name CLEARLY in the space above
3. Complete the form and submit a photo of this entire page
4. You or your friend can download the ebook to your preferred device

ISBN 9781631957390 paperback
ISBN 9781631957406 ebook
Library of Congress Control Number:
2021945148

Cover Design by:
Rachel Lopez
www.r2cdesign.com

Interior Design by:
Christopher Kirk
www.GFSstudio.com

Morgan James PUBLISHING **Builds** with... **Habitat for Humanity®** Peninsula and Greater Williamsburg

Morgan James is a proud partner of Habitat for Humanity Peninsula and Greater Williamsburg. Partners in building since 2006.

Get involved today! Visit MorganJamesPublishing.com/giving-back

For Betty Routliffe
No one has encouraged as many women as Aunt Bet.
She loves Jesus and treasures the rest of us like nobody's business.

Contents

Acknowledgments

I want to thank my husband, Ricky, who has supported this venture and stood by me through the ups and downs of menopausal emotions and the crazy freakshow life he helped create.

I also want to thank my sisters from other misters—Cathy, Steph, and Holly—who prayed their little butts off and believed God could do amazing things through us.

Thank you, Pastor Doug Blair, for keeping an eye on the stories to ensure we didn't lead anyone in the wrong direction.

I am forever grateful to Amanda Rooker at Split Seed Media, who exercised her sharp eye for detail while allowing my voice to shine through.

And thanks to the team at Morgan James Publishing, who were almost as excited as we were about this project. Their encouragement and expertise in every area were paramount to this book becoming a reality.

Introduction

Although I asked God into my heart at age seven, let me tell you, my adult life in no way reflected the "Join the Jesus Team" brochure. I've been married four times (twice to the same guy), boast a blended family of eight kids, and never once qualified for Mother of the Year. I've crawled back to God with a face full of tears, only to wander away time after time. And despite it all—or just maybe because of it all—I've seen God use me to encourage women. He welcomed me back, chose to forget the past, and helps me to live in victory day by day. Sister, I hope that these embarrassingly true stories will cause you to smile, reflect, and trust God in your own freakshow.

The Corn Crib

O f course, I forget the date or even the exact year, but I remember the feeling like it was yesterday. I was raised on a farm, 15ᵗʰ Sideroad, a mile from town. I remember long grass, gravel roads, cows chewing their cud, and angry geese chasing us around when we got too close. The nearest house was a long walk away, and childhood friends were sparse. Brothers were all I had, but mine were younger than me and altogether annoying. Back then, parents didn't entertain kids, and we made our own fun. The farm was a good place to grow up and learn the lessons of youth, but this particular lesson took fifty years to understand.

In the centre of the barnyard stood a dauntingly tall structure of wood slats and wire: the corn crib. As that little girl stared up at the sky-high mountain of cobs, unable to see the top, I immediately knew I needed to climb it. What fun I would have! I could climb to the moon. The excitement rose in my chest as I imagined it. My head buzzed with the prospect of the great climb. The boring days were gone, and the thrill of anticipation reigned.

My daddy did not share that same excitement.

"No."

Anger burned within me at the injustice of it all. *Why not? That's not fair! I mean, it's staring at me, just begging to be climbed. And I reeeeeeeally want to climb it.*

"No."

Anger turned to sadness and sadness to self-pity. My daddy didn't love me. Wouldn't a daddy who loved his little girl let her climb a glorious tower of corn cobs on a hot summer day? My tiny heart was crushed. I doubted my father had my best interest in mind, and I suspected he was out to ruin my fun and perhaps my whole life. Four-year-old girls can be tiny drama queens.

Many years later, as I sat with my dad in his last days of life on this earth, we reminisced about the good old days. We talked about the farm and all the fun we had.

"I do have a bone to pick with you," I teased.

I reminded him of his terrible treatment of his little girl. How could he have been so cruel? He refused to give me the very thing that my heart desired, the thing that would have made me happy on that hot summer day.

"Tess . . . there were *rats* in the corn crib."

Rats? Nooooo!

Suddenly, I understood. And I could clearly see that my father was protecting me, not denying me. He loved me very much.

Have you ever felt like this, like you wanted something so very badly and that thing you wanted was surely a good thing? Yet God would *not* say yes. It made no sense. You yearned for it, asked, begged, and tried to convince God it was a good plan.

Still, He said "no."

I get it. I've heard a hard *no* for many more serious things too. Sometimes we learn why, and sometimes we won't know for a long time—maybe not until we see Jesus face to face. But what I do know is that God loves us.

God sees today and the future at the same time. He knows every detail we are not privy to. The hard *no* sometimes doesn't make sense today, but we can know that God loves us. He is watching out for us in ways we can't even imagine. Trust Him.

Matthew 10:29–30 says, "Are not two sparrows sold for a penny? Yet not one of them will fall to the ground outside your Father's care. And even the very hairs of your head are all numbered."

Listen, Sister: What are you struggling to make sense of today? Tell God you trust He has His best in store for you. You are so very loved.

Winner, Winner, Chicken Dinner

L ately, I've been thinking back to a much busier time when I was up to my ears in kids and chores and making the most of days that flew right by. I recall four little boys horsing around and the fun of wrapping the day-to-day events of our family into an educational experience and calling it "homeschool."

Girlfriend, this was right up my alley. I thrive on deadlines, making lists, and meeting goals. I love being a mom, and spending oodles of time together certainly provided lots of great memories, including some of the best adventures in our little pop-up trailer.

One weekend, we arrived at our campsite with a van full of excited kids, supplies, food, and, of course, well-laid plans. If the kids would just cooperate, their dad and I could pop up the tent, unload everything, and set up camp.

This didn't seem like a lot to ask, but if you have ever spent time with children, you know that they are primarily little make-work projects.

"I need a drink."

"He hit me."

"I'm hungry."

I knew it was getting close to mealtime, so I tried to stave off their hunger with fruit using my famous "have an apple" response as I rushed to get things set up and stay on schedule. Dinner could not happen until we were all ready. I had a plan.

Finally, we unloaded the van and put away the food. I pulled out my neatly handwritten menu and examined it with pride and anticipation. I had outlined every meal and every snack in detail. It was neatly printed with headings underlined in red.

The boys watched impatiently as their dad searched through the gear for the barbecue lighter. Finally, lighter in hand, he opened the barbeque and *voila*! A chicken. From last summer.

Although there was no smell, the inside of the barbeque clearly indicated it had housed a good-sized hen for the last ten months. There was no saving this barbecue—or the chicken for that matter.

My meticulous plan was no help at all. I felt so frustrated. All my hard work was designed to avoid chaos, but instead of a well-organized "Dinner, Day One" we faced a trip to town with a bunch of hungry kids in search of a hardware store and Plan B for supper.

Are you like me? Are you rattled when things don't go the way you anticipated? Do you desperately long to know the next step?

I wonder if we've all been tricked into believing we knew what the days and years ahead would look like. We did a lot of careful planning for our futures and made assumptions of how they would play out. And, *whammo*, suddenly we're reminded that not one of us can predict with any accuracy what lies ahead.

People have always made clever plans that sometimes ended in disappointment: saving for retirement only to never see it, counting years at jobs that end earlier than expected.

Sometimes life changes in ways we can't predict. But do you know what? We know who can predict the days to come. So, here's some truth for today from Deuteronomy 31:6:

"Be strong. Take courage. Don't be intimidated. Don't give them a second thought because God, your God, is striding ahead of you. He's right there with you. He won't let you down; he won't leave you" (MSG).

Listen, Sister: Keep this truth circling in your brain and remember it when you are rattled. We may not know what the future holds, but we know who holds the future.

We Are Family

ears ago, my brother Bones decided to pop in at my place for a visit, unannounced. I'm definitely a fan of the pop-in. I love surprise visits, especially from family, but this visit would be one he would later regret.

Arriving at our little cul-de-sac, my brother noticed my spunky red Escort missing from the driveway. Bear in mind, this was mid-afternoon on a weekday, and the most exciting thing on my agenda most days was a trip to the grocery store. I was never gone long. Regardless, the door was locked.

Back in those days, we had no cell phones and carried on with our lives without the need to reveal our location twenty-four hours a day, every day. Today, this way of life sounds both weird and glorious.

Deciding to wait, Bones wandered the backyard, peeking in the windows and eventually becoming impatient. Considering my brother's personality at that time, I suspect somewhere around seven minutes had passed.

Standing in my flower garden, he hoisted himself up the brick and through the small opening in my front kitchen window. In broad daylight, in a busy cul-de-sac, my brother let himself into my house. Here's where things got interesting.

His head buried deep in the refrigerator searching for a snack, he missed the sound of approaching officers, sirens blazing. Imagine his surprise as he answered the door to a couple of our city's finest. Cruiser doors ajar and lights flashing, the cops rushed the door, confident they had foiled a "Break and Enter" in progress.

My brother fumbled for words, urgently trying to explain himself: he was no run of the mill thief; he was family. Of course, the experienced officers would have none of it. Tensions mounted as he told his story, attempting to persuade them of his innocence. Each time he repeated his explanation, the words came more quickly and emphatically, running together as beads of sweat lined his forehead. Pleading his innocence, Bones desperately wished for his sister to walk in the door at any minute, vouching for his innocence and confirming their connection.

Suddenly, it clicked. Leading them to an adjacent room, Bones directed them to a photo on the wall.

"This," he said, pointing at the picture, "is my sister, and this guy beside her is me." Proof positive.

As Christians, we're all brothers and sisters in one huge family. I'm wondering, though, how difficult is it for people to believe that we're part of the family of God?

If someone hears we're a Christian, are they surprised or shocked? I'm not talking about whether we have the "I heart Jesus" T-shirt or a regular parking spot on Sunday mornings. I'm referring to what they see in our character, our demeanor. Do we look like God?

Sometimes people get caught up in following rules. They get bent out of shape about implementing dress codes or making sure special words are recited. Maybe we need to wear dresses or a big square lace collar. Maybe there's expectations about hats or no hats. That's not what I'm talking about either. I don't think God cares about what we wear, eat, or drive. He cares about our heart.

If our heart is aligned to His, if our heart breaks for what breaks His, and if we earnestly want what He desires, we will begin to look more like Him.

And what would that look like? What does God want from us? The Bible tells us to love the Lord with all our heart, soul, and mind (Matthew

12:30), love people, show grace, (Colossians 4:6), and reply with gentleness (Galatians 5:23). Sounds easy peasy, right? Lord, have mercy! I need help over here. I want to blend right in for the family picture.

Galatians 5:22–23 says,

> "But the fruit of the Spirit is love, joy, peace, forbearance, kindness, goodness, faithfulness, gentleness and self-control. Against such things there is no law."

I want to be full of love, joy, peace, patience, kindness, goodness, faithfulness, gentleness, and self-control. And this is what God promises. Follow Him, and His Spirit will fill you with these.

Listen, Sister: How can you respond today with love, grace, and gentleness?

Tight

I t started out like most mornings, according to schedule. I woke with an early morning alarm, mentally marking things off my list and getting ready for work. And then one short phone call changed everything. People around here are still talking about it.

The call was a simple request from my sister in-law. A missionary family visiting from Australia was set to arrive at her house that afternoon, but my niece woke up to full-on stomach flu. It was the kind you really don't want to share a bathroom with, so their house was under quarantine.

Easy fix, I thought. I have oodles of room, and they were welcome to stay here. After hearing my sister's sigh of relief and settling the logistics, I hung up the phone and set out to quickly tidy up. Racing from room to room, I changed sheets and covertly stuffed laundry baskets of random articles into closets.

It was during this high-speed, ten-second tidy that I hit something I call the "space-time vortex." Girlfriend, have you ever run into this? One moment you have loads of time, and then, the very next, you have scarce seconds before you need to walk out the door. I had no time to lose. I threw my hair in a pony and began dressing, but when I reached for my black pants, I came up empty-handed. Immediately, a sense of panic filled my chest. I had just started a new job and had only one pair of work pants. Desperately searching my mind for clues, I suddenly remembered seeing them in the wash. I flew to the laundry room and grabbed the pants, climbing stairs two steps at a time. I was so relieved.

I was relieved, that is, until I started putting them on. I managed to slide my legs partway in, but when I tried pulling them up, I realized how much difference a few extra pounds could make. You see, my new job included a lot of sitting, and clearly my body was in full revolt.

I grabbed the belt loops securely and jumped, which seemed like a good idea at the time, successfully wedging my chubby thighs a little farther down into the leg holes. Now, here is where experience comes in handy, Girls. Thanks to my high school days, circa 1982, I knew that zipping these babies up would be more successful if I was in a horizontal position. I don't recall lying down being so uncomfortable in my teenage years, but time to reflect was not a luxury I could afford. I sucked it in for all I was worth and stood up, straight legged, and headed for the door.

The day that followed was like none other. After several unsuccessful attempts to climb up onto my lofty stool in my super-tight pants, I settled for backing up and leaning against it in an awkward, teetering position to greet incoming customers.

I didn't dare eat one bite of lunch in fear that another ounce might just blow my button clear off and wound a co-worker. I was newly inspired to lose some pounds.

As fate would have it, the new boss popped in for a surprise sales meeting in the boardroom. I took one look at the boardroom chairs and chose to stand. As awkward as that may have been for the others, I was both physically and emotionally uncomfortable, not to mention I had not peed all day. Oh, I wanted to pee; don't get me wrong. But I could not bring myself (literally) to lie down on the teeny, tiny bathroom floor to attempt round two of pant zipping.

I watched the clock in desperation, willing the hands to speed up. Five o'clock could not come swiftly enough, but finally, it was quitting time.

Racing home, I barely brought the car to a full stop as I rushed through the door to the bathroom. Sweet relief! Sitting down, I glanced at the label inside my pants. It read H&M. I didn't own pants from H&M. Only my twelve-year-old son wore their clothes.

And so, it dawned on me. I wore my son's pants to work. I was both relieved and embarrassed. He still refuses to talk about it to this day.

Obviously, I still talk about it occasionally because I believe it's important to laugh at ourselves.

We're told laughter strengthens our immune systems, diminishes pain, boosts our moods, and protects our bodies from the effects of stress. And Proverbs 17:22 tells us,

> "A cheerful heart is good medicine, but a crushed spirit dries up the bones."

By taking every opportunity to laugh, we can improve our emotional health, strengthen relationships, and even add years to our lives—years and years of funny, awkward stories. My son cannot wait.

Listen, Sister: Laughter is fun and healthy. Take time to laugh today.

Words of Hope

You can learn a lot about a person by seeing the front of their fridge. I've had an index card stuck to my refrigerator for many years. It's not a pretty recipe card from a new bride's box of tasty meal ideas. No whimsical flowery border or country chic design adorns it. Rather, the card is stained, battered, and worn. It's been clutched and crumpled, held tight, and thrown to the side. It's a lot like me.

I've always found the older, beat-up things most appealing. Time after time, I choose the vintage piece with a history of its own over the newest IKEA product. And, Sister, this card tells a story.

Between the lines is written a verse that breathed sweet air into my lungs at precisely the right moment and many moments since:

> I have loved you with an everlasting love;
> Therefore I have drawn you with lovingkindness.
> Again I will build you and you will be rebuilt,
> O virgin of Israel!
> Again you will take up your tambourines,
> And go forth to the dances of the merrymakers (Jer. 31:3-4).

A good friend gave me this verse at a time when my entire life was unraveling. Like a freight train out of control, I could see the damage before it happened, but I was powerless to stop it.

My marriage, once hanging precariously from a thread, smashed into a million slivers of shattered glass as I watched him walk out the door. My world was stifling, thick with grief. Intense fear and anger weighed me down. The future was charcoal black, and it was all I could do to lift my head from the green bedroom carpet.

My friend and I spent hours on the phone, sobbing, praying, and reminding each other (and ourselves) of God's promises. But as tightly as I gripped the card in my hand, I struggled to hold the truth in my heart.

I desperately wanted to believe it. But I couldn't see it. All I could see was darkness, shattered dreams, broken promises, and unending pain.

So, I read it. Over and over, I read these words of God. Out loud and whispered quietly, I read it. Sometimes I read it with angry shouts echoing in the dark; other times, I read with pleading questions through streaming tears.

And listen, Sister, nothing changed overnight. But God reminded me, day in and day out, of His truth. He showed up. He healed me. And I realized I never knelt on that green carpet alone. He was there. He was listening, drawing me to Himself. He was building me up.

Today, I turned the card over and noticed the date: May 2, 2013. Since 2013, I have been separated, divorced, and remarried (all to the same guy). I've watched two sons get married, seven grandkids come on scene, and my own dad die. And God has *always* been faithful—as only He can be.

This we know to be true: as Jeremiah 31:4 says, someday you will join me with our tambourines, dancing with the joyful.

Listen, Sister: Are you weary of fighting a difficult battle? Do you know a world heavy with darkness and fear? Remember, God is faithful. Fill your head with this truth today.

Look the Part

My ex-mother-in-law was a saint. She loved the boys like nobody's business, even though our kids rounded out her grandchildren tally somewhere around eighteen. She always kept a bag of jujubes in her purse, telling the kids, "You can have three," in her thick Dutch accent, rolling her *R*s. She always had time to snuggle, but she was also focused and organized. Her home was immaculate. Oh, how I respected that woman. As I watched her in admiration, I truly wanted to follow in her footsteps when I grew up. Because, in many ways, twenty-five isn't grown up at all.

As a young mom who hadn't slept through the night in somewhere around a hundred years, I felt more than a bit intimidated. I longed for her approval amid cultural differences, but I continually missed the mark I set for myself, despite my best attempts. But she was kind and dripped sweetness like honey, coming to my rescue time after time.

Her family was her life, and she was devoted, heart and soul. A homemaker by profession, she ran a tight ship. Mondays were laundry; Tuesdays were ironing; and so on. Listen, I live for structure, Girlfriend. I loved this so much; I feel giddy inside just thinking about it. Her house was clean and peaceful, and my tender heart aspired to these virtues. Of course, one blaring difference between our homes was the absence of four little toe-heads and their path of destruction on her white broadloom.

Striving to hold it all together, I worked hard to look the part of a well-organized mom who didn't just serve Fruit Loops for dinner. But no matter how hard I tried, I couldn't pull it off.

I thought, *Maybe if I stay up late, I can clean and organize the closets at night.* Who was I kidding? I could barely keep my eyes open to finish the bedtime story at seven o'clock.

So, in desperation, I became an expert at "hide and stuff", the game where dishes, messes, and laundry were magically ditched into any random orifice—closet, cupboard, or oven—as company came to the door. The charade continued for months, wearing me out as I barely held on by a thread. On the outside, I had a peaceful, organized-looking life, but on the inside, I felt turmoil, insecurity, and strife.

One evening, my mother-in-law popped by just as I was getting Curt out of the tub. The little guy's eyes lit up when he heard her voice, and he gladly let her towel him dry while I continued the baths.

"I'll help you get ready," she offered. "Where does your mom keep your pyjamas?"

My son answered his grandma back without hesitation, "In the dryer."

Lord, have mercy.

I'm sure she knew the struggle was real. She had raised five of her own. And I bet her baby-raising house wasn't perfect all the time—or maybe it was. She was amazing.

You see, she wasn't expecting me to be perfect or organized or anything other than who I was. This requirement was a lie I made up in my head, and the constant nagging was wearing me down. My own insecurity nattered at me, day in, day out, convincing me I was a loser. Girlfriend, the comparison game is always unfair. You will never win.

Girlfriend, we women are all the same. We all have a messy spot, a place we hide out of sight from others. Sometimes that's in my bedroom, and sometimes it's in my heart. Actually, it's often both, simultaneously.

Girlfriend, when your Sister is feeling all balled up inside, remember this truth.

> "Therefore encourage one another and build each other up, just as in fact you are doing" (1 Thess. 5:11).

Listen, Sister: Do you ever feel like you don't measure up? Does your heart yearn for the uncomplicated life? Do you desire the picture-perfect front porch post on Instagram? Remember, my friend, a basket of laundry is piled just inside that front door. Take a step back. Be real. Encourage others.

The Prints Match

I remember a time back in the "freakshow era" when my husband Ricky cleaned the bathroom. I'm sure he did it other times, too, but this time it caused quite a commotion.

Finishing the dreadful job, he restored all the cleaning supplies to their rightful places (the second sure sign of a good spouse) and returned to enjoy the luxury of an exquisitely clean restroom.

Believe me when I tell you, with a plethora of small boys in the house, a clean toilet was an absolute treasure. As the sole female on site, I did not understand how they continually missed the mark. It's not rocket science, boys. I encouraged their efforts, added cheerios to the toilet water to inspire attention to target, praised accuracy, and even forced a child labour schedule of periphery cleaning to remind them to aim. In the end, I'm not aware of the success of any of these strategies. Perhaps girls are just better with directions.

Back in the gloriously clean bathroom, Ricky washed his hands and glanced up into the recently polished mirror. Staring right back at him was a big, nasty smudge.

The frustrating defilement was not wayward splatter from an eager flosser or even soap bubbles whisked from hurried hands. Staring back in his face was the perfectly formed, soap-encrusted handprint of a small child.

Frustrated with the pointless duty of bathroom cleaning in a houseful of boys, my husband rallied the troops. Now, if you're a parent, or have ever been a child, you will not be surprised to learn that even under intense interrogation, the boys claimed "nobody" did it. Not one kid fessed up to the incident. More remarkable, no child stepped up to rat out one of his brothers.

Here is where my hubby's professional training in law enforcement came in handy. Lining the boys up, smallest to largest, he led them one by one into the bathroom and had them place their little hands on the soapy handprint. And guess what? Before we could even get to the guilty party, we knew without a doubt who had made their mark.

As the smallest guy's hand was enveloped by the size of the print, we watched a dire realization dawn on the face of his older brother. Fear mingled with regret as tears poured from his little eyes. The handprint would not lie.

Handprints tell a story. When you think about it, our peeps travel through life wearing our handprints. We've given them a hand of acceptance or rejection; we've pointed a finger of blame or offered a loving hand of understanding and grace.

Have you ever thought that we're covered by the handprints of God? He moulded us into being with His own loving hands. And He didn't stop there; He's relentless. While He never changes, we do. As Isaiah 64:8 tells us,

He works on us continually, softening the clay of our hard hearts, shaping us and molding us: "Yet you, Lord, are our Father. We are the clay, you are the potter; we are all the work of your hand."

Listen, Sister: Remember that He has changed you. He's patient and loving, constantly reshaping you into your new self: guiltless, grace-filled, and free. Hallelujah! Thank Him today.

Under Pressure

When I was a kid, my mom taught ceramics classes. Our basement hosted shelves of paints, greenware, plaster molds, and a kiln. Weekly, she welcomed women of all ages to sip tea and create masterpieces—if you call a frog who holds your scrubber a masterpiece.

The process started with pouring pails of liquid mud into molds and then leaving them for a time. Once removed, the hollow piece was cleaned with a sharp tool to remove rough edges and seams. Layers of paint were gingerly applied according to the artist's whimsy, creating grey matte laden with tiny chunks of hidden colour longing to explode.

Ugly, fragile, and useless, the hopeful projects were carefully placed in the kiln and fired at two thousand degrees.

The result, of course, was hard, durable pottery able to withstand a pelting spray and scrubbing bristles. The pieces, bright and smooth with glaze, were exquisite beauty to behold. But not one of us appreciates the intense pressure required to create that beauty.

I recall a particularly difficult season when I was battling every waking moment for our marriage, for our family. Overwhelming fear and anxiety left me crumpled and sobbing on the green carpet of my bedroom floor. Day after day, I was brought to my knees in my own weakness.

It was there, completely emptied, that I clung to God for every breath. Good friends prayed for me and with me, wisely counseling me to grab onto Jesus. And they reminded me to breathe, one day, one hour, sometimes one minute at a time.

Life felt too heavy. I couldn't clearly see a way out of the darkness as hopelessness settled into my bones.

Now, years later, that fiery kiln in my life has cooled. If I step back for a moment, I can see evidence that through the terrible, intense trial, God made me stronger.

There, on the green carpet, clutching Him for dear life, I breathed. I clung to His words, His promises. And He gave me *His* strength.

James instructs us in our suffering:

"Consider it pure joy, my brothers and sisters, whenever you face trials of many kinds, because you know that the testing of your faith produces perseverance. Let perseverance finish its work so that you may be mature and complete, not lacking anything" (Jas. 1:2–4).

Even if you don't find yourself in the kiln today, I bet one of your friends is feeling the heat. Pray for her. Encourage her. Remind her of her hope for the future.

And thank God for the beautiful masterpiece He is creating.

Listen, Sister: Maybe you feel a suffocating, intense pressure. Life seems hopeless. The stress is too much. Please know your heavenly Father is right beside you, leaning over you, longing to comfort you. He's ready for you to ask, to reach for Him.

Tagged

A few years ago, a friend approached my husband in the lobby of our local arena. It was just two red-blooded hockey dads shooting the breeze between periods.

"New jeans?"

"Ya."

Stop right there. Friends, I don't know about your man, but my hubby is no fashionista. He's not a fan of *Project Runway* or a subscriber to *Vogue*. Come to think about it, I had never overheard him speak a word about clothing design or popular trends. Perhaps this should have been the first clue.

"What are they, 34 x 30?" his buddy continued.

What in the world?

Soon, we discovered the tell-tale jean label stuck to the leg of Ricky's new pants, advertising his girth for all the world to see. Less troubling for a guy, it seems. I'd die.

Has this ever happened to you? You exit an event and learn hours later that you're still sporting the nifty "Hi, my name is _____" sticker, left chest.

That's the thing about labels. They don't always fall away; we must intentionally peel them off.

What labels are you wearing today? Mom? Friend? First-born? Listener? Debater? Failure? We all wear them, invisible to the naked eye yet powerful to sway our self-concept.

Without much thought, we stick these tags on ourselves and others. They may be birthed in reality, but oftentimes, I'm tempted to associate misplaced traits to these descriptors.

Follow me here:

Divorced = Unlovable

Older = Out of Touch

Unemployed = Loser

Infertile = Hopeless

Bored = Rejected

Do you get the picture?

Girlfriend, our situation does not determine our identity. By rights, the One who created us gets to decide who we are.

Imagine moulding cool clay between your fingers, carefully and thoughtfully forming your work of art, patiently sculpting an intricate treasure. Does the masterpiece decide its own identity? Of course not. The designer himself determines this.

God, our Creator, has decided who we are. Here are some remarkable labels He's given you:

- Fearfully and wonderfully made:

"I praise you because I am fearfully and wonderfully made; your works are wonderful, I know that full well" (Psalm 139:14).

- A new creation:

"Therefore, if anyone is in Christ, this person is a new creation. The old things passed away; behold, new things have come" (2 Cor. 5:17, NASB).

- Holy and dearly loved:

"Therefore, as God's chosen people, holy and dearly loved, clothe yourselves with compassion, kindness, humility, gentleness, and patience" (Col. 3:12).

- God's child:

"Yet to all who did receive him, to those who believed in his name, he gave the right to become children of God" (John 1:12).

- His workmanship:

"For we are God's handiwork, created in Christ Jesus to do good works, which God prepared in advance for us to do" (Eph. 2:10).

- Adopted:

"He predestined us to adoption as sons and daughters through Jesus Christ to Himself, according to the good pleasure of His will" (Eph. 1:5).

And so many more.
Hi, I'm Tess. Forgiven and free.

Listen, Sister: Let's inspect the tags we're wearing and compare them to what God says is true. As for the sticky, ugly labels that lie, we need to peel them off and replace them with bright, new accurate nametags. What does your nametag say?

Hitch It

Have you ever received a message from God? Have you felt a persuasive nudge, a calling in your heart to do a specific thing?

Now, I'm not talking about the sky opening or a thundering voice bellowing unmistakable instructions. Although indisputable, that method would be terrifying. I'd settle for a short email, simple Snapchat, or even a fiery bush in my path.

In my life, God sometimes talks to me internally, relentlessly prodding my spirit. When I'm unsure of His message or, honestly, when I don't want to listen, He patiently and persistently urges me forward. This was one of those days.

I was driving down a country road, on my way to the farm for an errand of some kind. The acres I once grew up on are now home to my grandkids, and any excuse is a good one to visit the little ones.

Just ahead, on the shoulder of the road, I noticed a frail, thin woman carrying a grimy green bag. It's so rare for someone to be walking that country road that I slowed to see if I might recognize the weary traveler.

Her hair was matted and stringy, and her clothing needed a good wash. She didn't glance up as I approached but continued to move slowly along the grassy ditch.

"Give her a ride." I heard God speak hot inside me.

Oh, no, no, no. That's not safe. I don't know her. Besides, I'm turning right, just up ahead. I have a list of things to do today, important things to accomplish.

Sadly, I'm quite experienced at these conversations, negotiating it would seem, with the One who created both driver and walker.

I did turn the corner up ahead and went about my day, totally forgetting about the poor girl plodding along the gravel road. I enjoyed lots of laughs with the grandkids, watching them roughhouse on the front grass until rain pelted hard and forced us to abandon the fun and games. Hours passed, and I needed to be on my way.

As I rounded the corner heading for home, I spotted her trudging slowly, soaked to the skin.

"Give her a ride."

Within seconds, my brain flooded with excuses. In my mind, I instantly spelled out the top-ten reasons to never pick up a hitchhiker. Yet the message persisted: "Give her a ride."

Reluctantly, I slowed to a crawl, inwardly hoping she would decline the invitation and I could be on my way. I mean, I would still get the points for obeying, wouldn't I?

Rolling down the window, I shouted through the deafening downpour, "Want a ride?"

As the wanderer buckled herself in, I noticed suffering had taken a toll on her body, adding undeserved years to her appearance. It hadn't been an easy life. Some of us live, and some merely survive. She didn't once look up, but I listened intently as bitter grief poured out, filling every crevice with her pain.

You see, her father had died the day before, and somehow she had scraped together enough money for a cab ride to his town, one way, a cab ride to see him one last time. And now she was going home, empty, alone, and defeated, in the pouring rain.

She didn't seem thankful for the ride. To be honest, I felt like she would have rather I plowed over her with my car. So much grief.

As I dropped her off and continued along my way, I thought about all the things I could have said or done for her. I could have offered food, money, or a hug. All I gave her was a ride and a listening ear. That's all I knew to do in that moment. And I must believe that if she needed more, God would have told me.

I'm still growing in this area of life, in obedience, listening, generosity, and love. And I'm thankful God is patient, waiting for me to surrender.

I'm convinced that if I didn't give the girl a ride, she would have still made the trip. But I would have missed the blessing: the blessing of generosity, the blessing of caring. And that I do not want to miss. Matthew 25:40 comes to mind:

"Truly I tell you, whatever you did for one of the least of these brothers and sisters of mine, you did for me."

Listen, Sister: Tune in to the persistent nudging of God today. Step out in faith and obey.

Like a Locomotive

I've had the same bra for three years, so I suppose it is time for a new one. Chris, the friendly lady at the bra boutique, urged me to come in for a fitting, and I cried. This took me by surprise. I cried at the thought of this gentle, kind lady measuring me. You see, the last time she took my measurements, a few years ago, it was to fit me for my first "adapted" bra after my mastectomy. At that time, it took weeks for me to work up the courage to go. She was so lovely and kind to me that I've been a repeat client for lots of other items since. I very much like her.

That's why the fear that gripped my heart and sprang unending tears down my face was so shocking. *Measure me? Like, with my shirt off? Umm . . . no.* This may not be rational, and I wrestle with that thought. But even my husband has not seen me naked for many months. Wait! Is this normal? Wow. Fear, how did you creep up on me like this? You're so comfortably nestled in my brain.

So, here's where the rubber meets the road. I'd been doing a lot of thinking and studying about our brains and the importance of filling our heads with truth. *Whammo.* Here was a chance to put my money where my mouth was.

Since I've been learning that our emotions are the product of our thoughts, I took a few quiet minutes to try to determine what kinds of things were running through my head feeding this intense fear with Ricky. Why was I so afraid? I was afraid that if he saw my body, he would know. He would see the ugly scar, the gross, flat, vacant chest. He would see my barren, empty, ridiculously awkward, and uneven appearance, my one poor, lonely breast missing her sister. It's just the weirdness of it all.

I'm ugly. I'm gross. And I've gained a few pounds, which is not helping me here, so let's add fat. I felt ugly, fat, and undesirable.

So, this line of thinking, like a locomotive out of control, was barrelling full throttle ahead and incessantly repeating in my brain. Circling the track, these thoughts went on and on and on. These thoughts produced feelings of sadness, worthlessness, and fear. Are you with me here? Can you relate? Recognize the emotion and backtrack to the thoughts that produced it.

But I have *good news*. There is hope. We can put on the brakes. We are not victims of our thoughts. We can choose.

I think the problem is distraction. I don't know about you, but about a zillion things are happening around me and in my mind at the same time. To me, this problem seems worse than with previous generations. Work, schedules, relationships, social media, food, music, and my phone are all swirling around in my mind. I'm constantly bombarded with expectations from work and family, and my cell is continually beeping notifications, texts, and calls. Not all of these are bad things, and some are necessary. But when was the last time you took even ten or twenty minutes entirely alone and quiet (no cellphone) to pray and connect with God, to meditate on His Word and listen? It's no wonder lies can settle into the corners of our brains and remain undetected for so long. By the time we take an honest inventory, they've been making the rounds for so long they've worn a rut in the road making it super easy for them to continue on and on. If we aren't careful, we'll allow lies to have a heyday in our brains.

Bad thinking affects our emotions. And emotions affect our actions, our relationships, and our consequences. Around and around we go.

The enemy is sly, but his tactics are not new. He takes God's promises and puts a question mark right at the end.

"Did God really say He'll never leave you?"

"Are you really a new creation?"

Over and over, doubt after doubt, these thoughts compound unconsciously in our brains. But once we recognize them, we can put on the brakes. We can take each thought and compare it to what God says. And—this is important—every lie must be *replaced* with truth.

Start with one big, fat lie. Each time you hear yourself think it, correct it. Speak the truth. The only thing we know to always be true is God's Word, so let's start there. Who does God say I am? Who are we according to Him? Second Corinthians 5:17 tells us,

"This means that anyone who belongs to Christ has become a new person. The old life is gone; a new life has begun." (NLT)

You are God's treasure. You are God's delight. You are valuable and deeply loved.

Listen, Sister: Find the truth and replace the lies. You have a choice. This is not easy. It's a battle. But it's one you will win with God's help.

Dancing Queen

Does the sound of a lively song set your toes tapping?

I spent most of my middle school years hunkered over the heating vent in our drafty, old farmhouse as George Jones crooned loud over the crackly transistor radio.

Dad was a jokester, and Mom shouldered a lifetime of teasing about her height, her cooking, and often her coffee-making ability, all in good fun. When she had suffered enough ribbing, she would shoot him "the look" and curtly tell him to "pound salt." I heard this expression repeatedly as a kid and often wondered how one could pound the teeny, tiny white granules. But since everyone around me seemed to understand, and no one else needed clarification, I just pretended to understand—a strategy I still use today.

Country music was ever-present in our early years, and when the DJ spun something from Hank or George or Johnny, we'd watch my dad gaze at his bride like a starry-eyed teenager. He'd grab her arm as she rushed to wipe her floury hands on her apron, and he'd whirl her around the uneven linoleum in her worn-out slippers.

There's something about keeping time with a song, isn't there? Whether you're a headbanger, a line dancer, a fox-trotter, or a talented guitar picker, we all love to connect with the beat. Moving to the music brings joy.

When my own kids were young, our large, open kitchen area was most often used as a wrestling arena, but it was also a mini sticks stadium, Hot Wheels raceway, and central living area for all the little people. But with the right song playing and the spirit moving us, Ricky would spin me around that dance floor to my heart's delight.

Personally, I'm a terrible dancer, and my kids have requested that I quit trying; they think I'm too old. Little do they know I've never been a great dancer; age has nothing to do with it.

From expressive dance to tapping your toe, it seems natural to sing and dance when we're joyful. I was reading this week about the wild party that took place after God delivered the Israelites across the Red Sea on dry ground. Can you even imagine? The snacks were nothing to write home about, but the celebration was second to none.

They were so grateful and full of delight that all the women took their tambourines and followed Miriam, dancing and singing. Sister, Miriam was a hundred years old! And when she was thankful, when she was filled with joy, she danced. You go, Girl!

Psalm 150:4 instructs us,

"Praise him with the tambourine and dancing; praise him with strings and flutes!" (NLT).

Listen, Sister: Are you thankful? Have you seen God answer prayer? Has He given you one more day to live and breathe? Use it to thank Him. Turn up the tunes and move your body. Tambourine optional.

Wall of Fire

For a time, I worked as the logistical coordinator at an industrial fire school. Okay, I made that title up. But for the record, my boss was well aware of my role and agreed this was an accurate description. I basically "put out fires" all day long. This was the perfect job for me and led me to experience something I will never forget.

Our school boasted bragging rights as the premier on-site industrial fire school in the country. The expansive training grounds offered life-sized props and mimicked possible refinery scenarios. The realistic live-fuel fires prepared the incoming workers for any impending emergency, and they loved it.

Local refineries enrolled their crews to be trained in on-the-job firefighting. Dressed in Nomex bunker gear, fire helmets with visors, boots, and safety gloves, the crew practiced a scene that could very well play out at work: a petro-chemical refinery on fire. How terrifying.

With students in place, our fuel technician opened the valve to pour propane through fuel lines and instantly ignite a twenty-foot towering inferno. The menacing orange flames roared and licked the sky as smoke billowed thick and black. Even with adequate gear, the heat was overpowering.

I'll never forget the scene. With a two-story wall of fire, red heat enveloped the metal frame, and smoke filled the atmosphere. Nothing else in life was of any consequence at that moment. The sight was breathtaking.

Did you know God describes Himself as our wall of fire? He is mighty, towering, magnificent, and all-powerful. What amazing protection He has over us. With this magnificent barricade shielding us, who can penetrate?

Sometimes I'm forgetful. I get fearful and worry about the future or even the present. I cower in fear, yearning for protection, fearful of the enemy. And God, our protector, steps right between us and our attacker and flicks his lighter, igniting a wall of fire.

Girlfriend, do you need reminders? I sure do. Calling this to mind is easier said than done; the enemy is sneaky. Trying to force us to lose hope, he attacks with a cancer diagnosis, unfaithful spouse, wayward children, job loss, addictions, and more. He tries to pile our minds high with insecurity, confusion, loneliness, guilt, and regret.

Remember, these fears are not from God; this is the enemy attacking. And between the attack and us, we find our defender, always on our side. He is our wall of fire. Sister, none of this defense depends on us. We don't supply the fuel, and we don't set the spark. We simply stand back and bask in His beautiful power.

In Zechariah 2:5, we read about this hope:

"'And I myself will be a wall of fire around it,' declares the Lord, 'and I will be its glory within.'"

Listen, Sister: Thank God today that He is your defender and rest in this truth.

Keep Tabs on Your Heart

I was cleaning out my bread drawer the other day, and my little brother came to mind—not because he's a neat freak (though he is) but because of his interesting childhood hobby.

As a small boy, my brother Bones (at one time a skinny, little jigger) had quite an impressive stockpile of bread tabs. Often you could find him sprawled out on the carpet, sorting mountains of plastic clips according to size and colour. He spent ages lying on the living room floor counting the treasure he had pilfered and scheming for more.

A mustard-yellow toy safe housed the prized collection, and a trusty combination lock warded off any would-be thieves.

The street value of the tabs was irrelevant. They were valuable to Bones. We knew this because he treated them like we all treat the things we treasure; he invested time in them, and he protected them/kept them safe.

This made me think about the things I value: Where do I spend my time? What do I strive to protect?

When I was a baby mama, all my waking hours—and weren't they *all* waking hours?—were spent caring for the children. I was on a mission to make sure they were safe and healthy.

Of course, parenting was a worthwhile venture. I hope I've taught my boys some important things by example, sometimes what to do, sometimes what not to do. And it seems natural to treasure our children. They're important to us and to God.

Now, I'm long past the toddler stage (thank you, sweet Jesus) and have only one son left to fly the coop. Teenagers sleep more hours than infants, so I have some extra time to play with over here. What am I doing with it?

We're told that where our treasure is, there we will find our heart. The two are tethered. *Yikes!* So, the way I spend my minutes reflects the contents of my heart.

1 Timothy 6:18 says we are to be rich in good works, generous with our time and money, and ready to share.

Friend, this is cause for serious reflection. God isn't finished with us yet.

Do you ever feel like your best years are behind you? Sometimes I do. But I'm learning that every season of life brings with it unique circumstances. And as long as He is giving us minutes, there are new opportunities.

Matthew 6:19–21 reminds us,

"Do not store up for yourselves treasures on earth, where moth and rust destroy, and where thieves break in and steal. But store up for yourselves treasures in heaven, where neither moth nor rust destroys, and where thieves do not break in or steal; for where your treasure is, there your heart will be also."

Listen, Sister: Do your best not to waste your day. Keep a watchful eye for every chance to love people. And who knows what you'll find next time you peer into the treasure chest of your heart.

Repulsive

I've never been the type of mom to overreact. If I spent hours with a kid in the doctor's waiting room, you can bet it was absolutely necessary. And this time, the visit was not only necessary but also an appointment we wouldn't soon forget.

It all started with bad breath. And I don't mean just your run-of-the-mill halitosis. I'm talking about a terrible odour radiating from our four-year-old's mouth. No amount of brushing, flossing (under duress), or breath mints could override the stench.

After many weeks, I gave in and dragged the boy to our pediatrician.

"An infection," he assured me with his all-knowing I'm-a-doctor smile, and he promised that antibiotics would fix the lad right up. They didn't. We tried the whole gamut, one after the other, but none could rid him of the putrid smell.

Our son had no pain or discomfort at all. It was, in fact, the rest of us who suffered. Have you ever noticed that small children whisper into your face and not your ear?

At our wit's end, we were finally referred to a specialist. Shining his super-cool pen light up the boy's nose, he spotted the culprit. Next, and my eyes water at the memory, he inserted his slim, metal grabber tool so far up the nostril I was sure it came to rest on the surface of my son's brain. Latching on, the doctor slowly and deliberately dragged out a splotchy, slimy, grey-black wad.

Instantly, the entire examining room was filled with an oppressively sick odour. With great urgency, the doc sped from the office, gripping the prize outstretched far from his body. He rushed out of the examining room, out of the clinic, and clear to the curbside garbage.

Returning to us, and looking rather unwell I might add, he explained his findings. The culprit was a Band-Aid in a tight ball, way, way up the boy's nose.

Goodness knows why, how, or when this had happened as no recent injuries could be recalled.

Girlfriend, aren't we sometimes like my little boy? We have something festering deep inside us and may not even be aware. Maybe it's easier for others to notice the foul odour exuding at inopportune moments.

Anger, jealousy, and unforgiveness can get tucked away, wound up tightly and perhaps forgotten. But with a bump or a jostle, the stink barges in, uninvited, a rancid influence in our words and reactions. It flows out into the room, an uninhibited stench that nobody misses.

This reminds me the wisdom found in Luke 6:45:

"A good man brings good things out of the good stored up in his heart, and an evil man brings evil things out of the evil stored up in his heart. For the mouth speaks what the heart is full of."

Out of the overflow of our hearts, our mouths speak. My good friend Cheryl taught me this. When my glass is bumped, the contents will spill. If our hearts are full of bitterness, it is bitterness that naturally slips out when life rattles us.

Listen, Sister: Let's get rid of these putrid things.

- Pay attention to the Spirit and what He is telling you.

- Recognize where you're going wrong and ask Him for forgiveness.
- Ask God if you are holding a grudge against anyone. Is there any offense unforgiven?

Like a rotting Band-Aid, remove it. With God's help, you can forgive. He will freshen up our hearts and sweeten our speech, like a cool, fresh breath mint.

I Dream of Genie

Raising kids is a daunting task, whatever stage you're in. After over thirty years of parenting children, I thought we were finally nearing the finish line. I heard the roar of the crowd, felt the well-trod path meet my tired feet, and savoured the aroma of roasted hotdogs filling the air—because every celebration deserves barbecued wieners, Sister. But no. Over the crest of the hill, the course sprawls on endlessly before my eyes; no parenting relief in sight.

My combined experience, both as a teenager (so long ago) and as a parent, has taught me one key point: parents know nothing. Thankfully, I've been working this gig long enough to see it consistently even out. Without exception, moms and dads become smarter, and by the time the child enters his mid-twenties, we've all but caught up.

Even though my sons span in age over eighteen years—a weird and not well-thought-out strategy—they all use the same basic techniques in interacting with us, "the 'rents." I'm not sure if these tactics are formally passed down like outgrown sneakers and ill-fitting blue jeans or if, perhaps, they are universally accepted schemes among youth everywhere. I can only speak from experience with my eight, but this feels like enough.

Currently, our youngest is perfecting the "genie strategy." As a rule, he spends every spare moment with friends, physically or virtually. He loves to cruise all over the county, racking up miles on the family car. When home, he barricades himself in his room and spurns invitations for engagement, board games, and meaningful conversations.

But on rare occasions, our son will slink out of his bedroom habitat, shirking the dirty dishes and fermenting gym socks, and nonchalantly sidle into a conversation or activity already underway in another room. Believe me when I tell you, he has gone so far as to slip into our bedroom and sit right on the foot of our bed. He engaged in meaningful conversation, noticed a new blanket, and rubbed my foot, however briefly. With my heart at ease and my confidence boosted, I dreamed of days ahead and reminded myself these years are fleeting. There is hope.

And then, with our guards adequately lowered, he swooned in for "the ask."

"So, there's a really cool pair of sneakers . . ."

Bam! A sneaky but brilliant tactic.

Girlfriend, do we do this to God? Are we less interested in the relationship and more concerned with the ask? Dear Lord, yada, yada, *ask*, amen.

I think we're all guilty of this at times. Instead of enjoying a close, personal connection with our heavenly Father, we treat Him like a magic genie and list our wishes. Thankfully, God is on to us. He loves us despite our selfish techniques and invites us into close communication with Him. God loves us so much that He longs for us to know Him better. He wants us to spend time with Him. He even lets us plan it according to our own schedule. But let's remember the promise in Psalm 91:1:

"Whoever dwells in the shelter of the Most High will rest in the shadow of the Almighty."

Listen, Sister: Intentionally spend time with the Lord today, in thankfulness.

A Bump in the Road

I've learned a great deal from my husband, even if it took a couple of tries to make our marriage stick. Our bumpy road was not my original plan; I can tell you that. But by the grace of God alone, here we are. In some ways, we've sort of melded together, as couples do, finishing each other's sentences. I can predict his reaction to any given situation with bullseye accuracy, and his memories have become mine after hearing his childhood stories many, many, many times.

Ricky grew up in a charming lakeside town in northern Ontario. Instead of a stony dirt driveway, he enjoyed the luxury of a real paved sidewalk right out front. Jealous.

Just down the street, an enormous maple overlooked the neighbour-hood, providing much-needed shade and a spectacle of fall colors. But the tree also brought with it quite a disturbance. Eventually, the roots worked their way up beneath the sidewalk, causing the cement to buckle. The resulting uneven path was a dangerous obstacle and an eyesore for anyone, like me, whose brain adores straight lines and smooth paths.

I imagine the disappointment of the city workers who laid that cement. After leveling the ground, spreading gravel, building forms, and carefully adjusting the slope, they stood back admiring their handiwork. Perhaps they imagined the bustle of ladies, purses in hand, hurrying their way to the bank or clusters of Levi-clad teenagers sauntering along or starry-eyed couples strolling in the moonlight down their carefully leveled walkway. And yet the mighty maple had another plan.

For three-year-old Ricky, this uneven bulge in the path was pure glory. Day after day, the little tyke would mount his squeaky, red tricycle. With reckless abandon, he pedaled his little heart out, the wind in his hair, hitting that crack at full speed and losing touch with the ground for a split second. Sweet air!

Oh, the pure delight that filled this young boy's heart, all because of a bump in the road.

Isn't that life? We have expectations; we have built the thing, planned, leveled, and looked forward to smooth sailing. And then life happens. Things change, and up springs a bump in the road. Our vision for the future is shattered. Our plan is skewed; our expectations are crushed.

My friend, I'm reminded that you and I are not the master builder. God has the best plan, and He is well aware of the road ahead. Often, I long to look at His blueprints, to learn the next step and take a sneak peek around the corner. But would I really want that? Girlfriend, if I had seen the road ahead, if somehow I was granted a forward glance a few years ago, I would have been scared skinny. And yet He has brought me through every trial, through family strife, sickness, and mourning, and He has given me abundant peace and the closest walk with Him.

We can be sure that God promises to never leave our side. I picture Him standing on the rear deck of the tricycle, wind in His hair, egging us on to pedal harder and faster, and reveling in the chest-piercing thrill of ultimate joy as we hit that sweet air.

As we look back upon our bumpy roads or the jolting cracks in our cement, let us think on the promise in Proverbs 19:21:

"Many are the plans in a person's heart, but it is the Lord's purpose that prevails."

Listen, Sister: Reflect today on all the times God has been faithful while you navigate the bumps in the road.

Smarty Pants

I
f I had played my cards differently way back when, I could boast an impressive university education. But playing the "what-if" game is not helpful, and submitting to the feeling of insecurity is never a good thing. More than once, it has backfired in an awkward way.

I worked at a post-secondary institution where my colleagues were experts in their field and some of the most brilliant people you could ever meet. Most days, I loved my job and enjoyed chatting with my workmates. One morning my supervisor was droning on about politics or world history or something else that I'm not really interested in, and my lack of engagement probably showed on my face. He strolled back to his office with an air of superiority, and I immediately felt a familiar sick feeling smoldering in my chest.

As emotions overtook my common sense, I had a deep burning desire to prove myself. I desperately wanted him to recognize that I was not a loser. But, oh, I felt like a loser, someone uneducated, inarticulate, and unversed in current events and popular movies. I just felt dumb.

So, what did I do? I followed after him and initiated a whole new discussion, a do-over. I don't even remember the topic, but I do recall debating in a relatively intelligent manner for several minutes in the school lobby as a hundred or so students filed past us on their way to class. Many noticed me there, obviously impressed somehow by my witty conversation. They couldn't hear my words, but almost every one of them smiled broadly at me as they shuffled past.

Once I made my final point, I returned to my office with a sense of accomplishment. *See?* I thought to myself, *You are OK. You've got this. You are smart and well-spoken. You are impressive. He is astounded by your great wisdom.* I was on a bit of a roll by then.

A delivery had arrived while I was away from my desk, and as I glanced down at it, I spotted something not quite right out of the corner of my eye. It was my pants. Both pant pockets were pulled entirely inside out and had been drooping limply at my waist the entire morning. I flashed back to the grinning faces of all those students as they paraded past me in the lobby.

My recently found confidence hit the ground like a lead balloon. As my face flushed various shades of red, my mind filled to the brim with thoughts about myself—not one gentle or kind. To be honest, most were ideas that are usually running in the background of my mind anyway, just waiting their turn to be called to centre stage: *You're dumb. You always look stupid. You will likely end up losing this job.* And on and on the sad story goes.

What about you? What is on the playlist running in your head these days? I think most of us have a soundtrack of some sort playing on repeat in our minds. And this point is important: I get to create my playlist. *You* get to create yours.

You see, we are in a monumental battle, Friend, and that battle takes place right between our ears. The enemy is sly, but his tactics are not new: Feed us lies. Repeat. This was his strategy with Eve in the garden, and it's his strategy with you and me today.

Sometimes we don't even realize the ideas circling in our head are full-blown lies. We can be distracted by the busyness of life and never actually take a good inventory of our thoughts, but doing so is an important exercise, one that I encourage you to do.

A list of fresh new tracks in our mind will fill our thoughts with genuine truth. In Philippians 4:8 Paul speaks of being intentional with our thoughts:

"You'll do best by filling your minds and meditating on things true, noble, reputable, authentic, compelling, gracious—the best, not the worst; the beautiful, not the ugly; things to praise, not things to curse" (MSG).

Listen, Sister: You and I need to remember who we really are. The truth is, God says we are valuable to Him. We are His treasure and His delight. I think sometimes we even make Him smile.

According to Plan

Have you ever noticed the anticipation of a special event often outweighs the joy of the occasion itself?

I grew up pre-Snapchat and FaceTime, so, yes, I am old. Back in the day, we had two ways to connect with friends. The first was a party-line telephone attached to the kitchen wall. Perhaps you're thinking a party-line was some sort of call-in phone service where people connect, like a 1980s Tinder. It was not. A party-line was a landline shared by neighbours. We waited our turn to use the phone, and if a person was bored or mischievous or just nosey about the lives of the people next door, they (hypothetically speaking) listened in.

The only other option for connecting was in-person communication. My parents were ultra-strict, allowing me out socially only twice a month, so, Sister, you better believe those two days were precious to me.

In an unprecedented move, for my sixteenth birthday, my dad allowed me to attend one additional social function. Luckily, our youth group was planning a roller-skating event at a rink in the city, and I signed up before he could change his mind. For the next few weeks, my mind buzzed with anticipation, imagining dazzling lights bouncing off the revolving disco ball, the whir of fat skate wheels on the rubber floor, and Rick Springfield blaring from the speakers. I was pumped.

My mind was filled with thoughts of traveling to the city and hanging out with my besties. I had it planned out down to the last detail. I even purchased new socks. All of mine had brightly coloured little pompoms at the ankle, a fashion necessity in the '80s, and I was determined to skate in total comfort.

The day finally arrived, and according to schedule, carloads of teenagers rallied in our laneway to begin the trek. Elated, I bounded out of the house and toward a night of freedom. Everything was going according to schedule: hair feathered, check; blue jean shorts, check; new socks, check.

But wait. Something felt off. Instead of anxiously coaxing me into a seat, teenagers were spilling out like a clown car at a circus, making themselves comfortable on our lawn. Freezing in my tracks, I glanced back to see pure delight settle onto my mom's face.

She had pulled it off. For weeks, she had been planning a birthday party for me. Counting down the days, she had invited guests, made delicious snacks, and kept the secret.

I hate surprises. I like to schedule; I like to plan. I prefer to know what's going to happen with reasonable certainty. But have you noticed that God doesn't work that way? Have you, like me, offered up a well-organized list of ideas and suggestions and constructed a timeline that works for you?

Yet, it seems that He delights in surprising us. Often, God performs the miracle and answers the request when I least expect it. I picture Him planning a gala, a giant reveal, with every piece orchestrated down to a *T*. As I'm working things out in my head, desperately struggling to line things up on my end, my heavenly Father already has every meticulous detail arranged. And He is patiently waiting for the perfect moment to pull it off.

God gets a kick out of lavishing us with love:

"See what great love the Father has lavished on us, that we should be called children of God! And that is what we are! The reason the world does not know us is that it did not know him" (1 John 3:1).

And I think He takes great joy in that surprised look on our faces.

Listen, Sister: Ask God to surprise you with something unexpected today.

Reluctant Consent

ometimes a day that begins like any other can lead to choices that change eternity for someone you know. Let me tell you about just such a day.

My office building was "cleaned" by a lady named Ruth. I say "cleaned" because we once got a report of the lunchroom tables being wiped down with her wet mop. Ruth was quite a character. She smoked like a chimney, and I'd often come across her taking extended breaks on a wooden bench in the ladies' change room.

Life had not been gentle to this woman, and although she was a decade younger than me, she always seemed worn out, like the mop was holding her up as she shuffled down the hall. She was a quirky lady and didn't have many friends in the building, but I liked her. I relate well to the misfit.

One day Ruth approached me, worried stiff, awaiting results of a lung biopsy. She asked if I'd been upset when I received my cancer diagnosis; she wondered how I coped.

I told Ruth about the peace that comes with prayer and explained my relationship with Jesus and how He hears me and understands. With that, she went about her day. But not so with me.

As I returned to my duties, I felt God tell me, "You need to go and pray with her."

Let me tell you. I did *not* want to do it—not at my job, not in front of my co-workers. But God did not let up. He was relentless, and I knew it. So, I did the only thing I could do. I tried to bargain with God. If You bring her here into my office, where I can shut the door, *then* I will do it.

No dice.

As my workday wound down, I knew I needed to find my friend. And find her I did, in a huge, central meeting room surrounded by glass walls—the most conspicuous place in the building. And there I held her close, and we prayed, and she cried. She never returned to work.

Months passed until one day Ruth's husband showed up in my office. She had begged him to bring her, and the sight of my friend flooded my heart with compassion. She was unrecognizable. A hundred pounds lighter, bald, and weak, her poor body had been ravaged with the effects of chemotherapy. Again, we prayed, and as time passed, I visited her in palliative care where I had the privilege of sharing my faith and hope for eternity only a few days before her death.

I'm sharing this story *not* because I deserve any kind of pat on the back. Quite the contrary. I obeyed kicking and screaming all the way.

I want to encourage you. God *is* at work. He is doing amazing things all around us.

Is He prodding you today? Do you hear His quiet voice? Perhaps you know what He is asking. Maybe it's uncomfortable, scary even. Maybe, like me, you are trying to negotiate a deal with God, hoping for obedience on your terms.

Oh, Sister. Let's be women who listen. Let's be like Isaiah, who boldly responded to God's call:

"Then I heard the voice of the Lord, saying, 'Whom shall I send, and who will go for Us?' Then I said, 'Here am I. Send me!'" (Is. 6:8).

Listen, Sister: Is God asking you to do something for Him today? Do not delay.

One of the Cool Girls

I thought the desire to be one of the cool girls would wear off over time but apparently not. It's been forty years and counting over here.

A while back, I was working for a promotional advertising company, pedaling embossed pens, mugs, and team apparel. This was my jam. I liked rubbing elbows with clients and building relationships and felt confident in both the product and service I provided. Good times.

One summer night, I was slated to deliver a presentation to a local sports team. I set up in a boardroom with samples, quotes, and what I thought was a decent presentation. It was a small-town team, and I felt relatively comfortable—that is, until the committee rolled in.

The men on the board were inconsequential, to be honest. I don't remember if they existed. The women, however, were another story.

Close your eyes and picture, in slow motion with a gentle breeze fanning their satiny, straight hair, a parade of poised and confident young women boldly parading into the room. Girlfriend, I may not be in high school anymore, but as they took their seats, I glanced down at my department store skirt and somewhat matching blouse, and a whole host of awkward teenage feelings flooded back to their former residence in my brain.

On this side of the room, I present the sexy circle of Charlie's Angels, sharing secrets, flipping their hair, and smiling big with their ultra-white teeth. And to your left, the hot-mess express of Tess Scott. Or so it felt to me.

I muddled through the meeting and hurriedly packed up, bolting out of there lickety-split. If I could have taken a second to think, I would have realized the presentation itself hadn't been terrible. It seemed well-received, and just maybe I had pulled it off.

Outside, I dumped the bulky bags and leaned over, breathing a massive sigh of relief. The exhale of air reverberated between my cheeks, rippled across my lips, and made a crazy, loud "horse sound" on the way out. The unexpected vibration felt odd, so I practiced it a few times to perfect my method.

Just then, I heard a rustle behind me. As my chest filled with red-hot lava, I looked up to see Cool Girl Number One gawking at me from beside her car. Lord, have mercy.

I've since moved from that town. Though it was not because of the incident, I'm relieved all the same.

Girlfriend, the comparison game is a trap. Whether we compare our bodies, our talents, our families, or our Instagram-perfect kitchens, we all come out losers. Listen, our true identity comes only from our Creator. He gets to name us, to say who we were designed to be. And that has nothing to do with hair products and teeth whitener.

God made me exactly this way—sometimes fun, sometimes terribly awkward—to encourage other women along the way, so I take comfort in Romans 12:6:

"We have different gifts, according to the grace given to each of us."

Listen, Sister: What did He create you to do? What desires did He embed in your heart? Ask Him today.

Hairy Like My Dad

The first time I met our son TJ in the neonatal unit of our local hospital, I was a bit shocked. Our other sons had taken their sweet time to arrive on-scene, delivered into the world weighing somewhere in the seven-to-eight-pound category. This wee one was another story.

TJ was born eight weeks early and barely moved the scale at a meager four pounds. His translucent skin was covered by downy, soft hair, and his helpless, wee body lay uncovered and alone, attached to wires and tubes. What a battle he would have to fight, and fight he did.

As our little preemie grew into a smiley, curly-headed tyke, the hair covering most of his body darkened. And, boy, was he proud of it. Often, we'd hear him say, "I'm hairy like my dad."

The irony here is, TJ is adopted.

Growing up, I thought it would be amazing to be adopted. I had the impression that adoptive parents worked hard with great intentionality to add a bundle of joy to their family.

One of my childhood friends was adopted, and often I heard people mention how she looked like her sister. Sometimes she corrected people, and sometimes she didn't bother. Maybe it was comforting to know she fit into her family so seamlessly.

Physically, my friend really didn't look like her siblings, but she had taken on their mannerisms, their posture, and often the way they responded. Even her voice inflections were spot on.

Girlfriend, this right here is the reason we want our kids to hang out with "the right friends." Rubbing shoulders always results in rubbing off. Spending time together will no doubt mean one of you is rubbing off on the other.

When we begin a relationship with a new friend, it's natural to spend time with them, talk to them, ask them questions, and intentionally get to know them. It's the same with God. Spending that time getting to know Him will result in a change in us. We will become more like Jesus: more compassionate, more humble, more gracious, and more loving.

I'm thankful to be adopted into the family of God, and I hope He rubs off on me more and more as time goes on:

"He predestined us to adoption as sons and daughters through Jesus Christ to Himself, according to the good pleasure of His will" (Eph. 1:5, NASB).

Listen, Sister: God says you are adopted. What if the amount of time you spend with Him resulted in you "looking" more God-like? Intentionally spend time alone with Him today.

Plan A

We welcomed TJ into our bustling brood of boys as a foster brother, preparing our hearts for the inevitable. "You'll have him for a couple weeks," they told us. Little did we know.

Our little curly locks boy brought his share of joy and heartache to this boisterous family. As a toddler, he hit all the milestones you would expect, but he took his own sweet time getting there. I was less worried than I might have been. This was not my first mama-rodeo, and I knew kids eventually take their first step, say their first word. And he did.

He was diagnosed with Fetal Alcohol Spectrum Disorder (FASD) the same summer he learned to ride his two-wheeler without the training wheels. I remember the scene, the precise spot I was standing as my eyes poured hot tears of disappointment, outrage, and disbelief.

FASD is caused when the (birth) mother drinks alcohol during pregnancy. The resulting brain defect causes difficulties with memory, problem solving, and impulsivity. Generally, people with FASD struggle to attach consequences to their actions, and this is something our boy had been struggling with daily.

With this reality solidifying in my brain, the future I saw for our son dissolved into thin air. I watched helplessly as that doctor took the story of

TJ's life and violently ripped out the pages one by one, leaving crumpled wads of paper recklessly strewn about.

But those expectations, that life plan I had imagined in my mind as I rocked him on my knee and tucked him in at night, were only *my* plans. Nothing had really changed except my perception, my acknowledgment of the brutal truth right before my eyes.

To say life with FASD is challenging would be an understatement. TJ has fought battle after battle for over twenty years now. Few people understand this, perhaps least of all him. And just when I think he's in a good place, on a smooth road, the wheels fall off.

And like a monstrous explosion out of the blue, years later we found ourselves right back in crisis mode. Again, I was panic-stricken and worried sick. I hated my lack of control.

All comfortable routines, safe arrangements, and carefully crafted plans were chucked out the window. The total sum of all I knew about my boy's future was zero.

I wept and I pled for our son. I stomped and shook my head. I replayed my life, my parenting decisions—good, bad, and terrible—as I cowered to the enemy's blame game. Spiraling downwards into an all-too-familiar pit, I heard a faint word in the distance. A whisper, almost inaudible. Finally, an answer. "Trust Me."

God answers. He is not surprised. He wrote this book. His love is lavished on my boy; his love is lavished on me.

And I still grope to learn and trust Him more. Each day, I am one tiny step closer to taking Him at His Word.

How about you? Are you stressed by situations that seem out of your control? Does your future look entirely different than you had hoped?

Believe me when I tell you accepting my lack of control is something I am circling back to daily, hoping for forward motion and praying for growth. Maybe you can relate and take some encouragement in this process:

1. Acknowledge that God is always in control. Thank Him for this.

2. Hand Him everything. I try to visualize placing things (worries, people, problems) in His ginormous hands.
3. In place of the burden, receive in your outstretched hands the peace He promises to us.
4. Next, when you notice you have returned and plucked some things right back out of God's capable hands, return to step two.*

*I do not recommend step four. Avoid that step. I'm just being transparent here.

Girlfriend, I'm working on this, and I bet you are too. My mama heart is hurting, stretching, and hopefully growing closer to God every minute as I learn that I am never outside of His care.

"For I am convinced that neither death nor life, neither angels nor demons, neither the present nor the future, nor any powers, neither height nor depth, nor anything else in all creation, will be able to separate us from the love of God that is in Christ Jesus our Lord" (Rom. 8:38-39).

Listen, Sister: This life, your life, is God's Plan A. He is not surprised. And while you do not understand it, you can trust Him. He is in control.
Thank you, Jesus.

Left Turn Only

I saw a meme this week that said, "I love all of my kids equally, but there is that one I work extra hard to not wake up."

Raising a rather large family of boys, I've seen a gamut of personalities, strengths, and talents. No two kids are alike; that's for sure. As they grew, I loved spending time with each of them, and I clearly remember which was the easiest to entertain.

When TJ was a young boy, he preferred to play alone. His imagination knew no bounds, and he was quite happy living in his continuous world of make-believe. Most of the time, this worked just fine for the rest of us. For hours on end, he would amuse himself alone in the backyard, and Girlfriend, let me tell you, one kid not pestering the rest was a welcome shift in the family dynamic.

To the untrained eye peeking through our fence, it must have looked like a small boy sitting deserted in the grass under a rotting picnic table. Occasionally, the young lad climbed out and walked the circle around the table before retreating underneath again, repeating the cycle time after time.

But in TJ's world, that picnic table was a souped-up race car. He drove endless laps around the track, banking, driving flat out around the curves.

Every hundred rounds or so, he would pull into the pits, fuel up, change the rubber, and clean the windshield, obviously.

TJ inherited his love of racing from his oldest brother and naturally longed to follow in those giant footsteps. By his fourth birthday, he still had trouble reciting the alphabet but could rhyme off every driver, car number, and sponsor in the NASCAR circuit.

Soon, we realized the picnic table race car was more than a passing fancy. Ricky picked up an old steering wheel from the junkyard and leaned hubcaps, serving as make-shift tires, against the benches for pit stops along the way. This may have been for us more than him now that I think of it. He was just as content to hang out alone in the grass, with or without the props.

Let me assure you, in my defense, we did purchase real toys for the boy: dump trucks, balls, games, and bikes. There were brothers, neighbours, and schoolmates to play with, but time after time, he returned to the ground under the picnic table to play there alone.

Sister, sometimes I wonder if we are each sitting alone under our very own table while a life of purpose and joy awaits on the other side of the fence.

Maybe we're satisfied sitting there in the shade. It's dry and quiet, and the grass is comfortable. And maybe stepping out, away from what we know, is uncomfortable, even scary.

But here's the thing; God has called us to an amazing life. Girlfriend, can you feel it? We were made for more:

"For we are God's handiwork, created in Christ Jesus to do good works, which God prepared in advance for us to do" (Eph. 2:10).

Perhaps the problem is we're too easily satisfied. If I'm not careful, I can be content to live in my imagination, distracted from life and perpetually entertained. Day in, day out, I easily flood my mind with social media, Netflix, Instagram, TikTok—all a virtual world of escape.

But God offers so much more; He offers a calling on your life. He's ready to share it with you, to light that fire in your heart.

Listen, Sister: You can make a difference in the world, in the lives of other people, by spreading the good news and bringing hope. Stop driving in circles, going nowhere.

With Scars Come a Story

There's a nasty looking scar on the belly of my son Jesse. The jagged, vertical slice has faded over the years but remains nonetheless as a reminder of suffering, long since healed.

When people ask, he attempts to reel them into an unbelievable tale of adventure, saying he narrowly escaped death battling a hungry shark. The truth is, he doesn't remember where the scar came from as he was not quite two years old at the time.

We were sitting around a roaring campfire, patiently waiting for the fierce flames to smolder into hot embers, suitable for marshmallows (and subsequently s'mores—the only good reason for camping).

As Jesse toddled between our lawn chairs, he stumbled on uneven ground and plunged, seemingly in slow motion, right into the flames. Our two-year-old fell into a raging fire!

His dad reached in and plucked him out within seconds, though it felt longer, and we rushed to the tap, pouring cold water over his shivering body. His entire chest, stomach, leg, and foot were badly burned.

Camping in a remote area meant medical help was not close by, so gathering his siblings, we drove, like wildfire, to the nearest hospital. I'm sure we made record time, with his dad paying no regard to the law and me holding him on my lap as he clawed at the window and screamed bloody murder. I wanted to scream too. I will never forget watching his tender baby skin bubble and erupt before my eyes. It was a horrendous experience, and it left a scar.

Many of us are walking around with scars. Some scars are visible, some not, but all are acquired through pain.

We're familiar with the physical scars that result from a wound to our skin. They're excruciatingly painful at the onset, but with time, healing happens, leaving only a visible reminder and sometimes a cool story.

The tricky thing is, some of us wear our scars on the inside. Internal scars are harder to detect, yet they often affect our choices and behaviour for a lifetime. Emotional trauma can lead to many struggles:

- Inability to trust
- Sexual inadequacies
- Constant need for validation
- Low self-esteem
- Mental illness
- Emotional instability

I'm not a counselor, but I'm on this journey with you, and I've learned that transformation comes through acceptance and forgiveness.

So, whether you're healing internally or loving on people who are, ask God to help you bear in mind the unseen struggles of those around us. Let's offer grace instead of judgement and kindness instead of criticism.

Jesus suffered physical scars so that we could offer grace to those who struggle:

"But He was pierced for our offenses, He was crushed for our wrongdoings; The punishment for our well-being was laid upon Him, And by His wounds we are healed" (Is. 53:3, NASB).

Listen, Sister: I can't wait to meet Jesus face to face and feel His big bear hug around my neck. He'll still wear deep scars on His hands, evidence of the price He paid to heal the scars inside of me. If you've accepted His gift of salvation today, thank Him right now.

Men Are Not Women

Idon't know if you've given this any thought lately, but let me remind you of something: men are not women. I was hit square between the eyes with this powerful reminder just a few days ago.

My husband, bless his heart, was relaxing quietly at the kitchen table, minding his own business as I returned to our peaceful home.

My own brain had been swirling, replaying the day's events during my commute, so when I burst on scene, I may have resembled a rabid squirrel in a full-blown tizzy barging into the room.

Without so much as a friendly greeting, I vividly described recent events, including my struggle with a particularly difficult relationship, which I may or may not have mentioned to him daily in the past, *ad nauseam*.

With great passion and exuberant hand signals, I described my grievances. As the conversation rounded the corner for home, my eyes returned to the kitchen, and I noticed my husband still sitting in the same position, motionless.

He appeared to be (possibly) listening quietly, not uttering a word.

To his credit, he did not jump in to fix the situation. Oh, no, this man has some years of marriage under his belt. He said nothing—no head nod, no "mmhmm" in agreement. Nothing.

Sister, any girlfriend worth her weight would have understood my frustration. She would have known how to empathize, how to listen until the end, shaking her head in agreement and offering the precise balance of sisterly support, dislike for the culprit, and holy "we'll pray for him" solidarity.

To be clear, my hubby did nothing wrong. It was my expectations steering me south down a twisty, dark path of disappointment. And this was not my first tour on this particular path. If I'm honest, I'm a frequent visitor.

Time after time, I find myself baiting my husband, longing for affirmation of his everlasting devotion. I think, *Maybe this time he will give me the answer I'm dying to hear.* For instance, I might say, "I wish you still thought I was pretty."

To a man's ears, this sentence must sound like a statement of fact, like, "I wish the Toronto Maple Leafs won," or "I wish there was pie." But for a woman—or at least for me—it's an invitation left hanging, vulnerable, echoing in the dark. An unnerving appeal, cowering and exposed, yearning for confirmation, dreading certain rejection.

Listen, Sister, he's not being unkind. He seriously has no clue. He's a man. Here's a few things to keep in mind when dealing with their kind:

- Men don't worry that their sweater falls in the wrong spot on their torso.
- Men don't change their socks to match their shoes, leading to a change in pants, resulting in their shirt clashing and the unforeseen necessity of a whole new ensemble as he walks out the door.
- Men don't wonder if the extra ten pounds is noticeable on their hips.
- Men don't change their opinion depending on the day of the month.
- Men don't think about underlying tones and the seven things that a passing comment could have meant.

I'm trying to remember to adjust my expectations. I know my affirmation comes from my Creator alone. God created you and me with a longing only *He* can fill. He has already spoken over us with His great love. We are chosen and cherished beyond measure.

"Satisfy us in the morning with your unfailing love, that we may sing for joy and be glad all our days" (Ps. 90:14).

To be perfectly honest, I'm glad men are not women. I'm thankful my husband is rock solid and predictable. One woman over here is enough.

Listen, Sister: Are you looking to another person to meet a need that only God can fill?

Head Games

Have you ever had a random song stuck in your head?

It was mid-morning in my new "working from home life," and I caught myself singing, "Who's in the Wiggle house, who's in the Wiggle house, who's in the Wiggle house today?"

If you don't have littles at home or grand-littles visiting, you may not recognize the theme song of this popular kid's show. It's the equivalent of "The Song That Never Ends," that one-verse, infinitely repeating children's classic made popular by Shari Lewis and Lamb Chop back in the day: second verse same as the first.

Slightly embarrassed by my choice of music, I immediately looked around, wondering, *Who's in Tess's house?* But the little ditty played relentlessly in my head throughout the day, despite my best efforts to stop it.

I imagined a vintage record player, the needle reaching the centre and returning to its base in silence. Ah! Silence. Moments later, I was humming the tune again.

Isn't this always the way with our thought life? I'm often unaware of thoughts playing in the background of my mind. When at last I'm mindful of them, they've inevitably been nattering at me subconsciously, somewhere beneath the surface, for many moons.

Harmless (albeit annoying) jingles are sharing my head space with more dangerous thoughts, like full-blown lies the enemy has planted about my value, my future, and my past (long forgiven).

And believe me when I tell you that a post-cancer body is fertile ground for the enemy's deception, insecurities, fear, and worry.

Simply deciding to dismiss these thoughts has never worked for me. Have you ever had someone tell you *not* to think of an elephant? I bet you see his swaying trunk and floppy ears every time.

Let's assess the information we are shoveling into our minds in the first place. Personally, I have been guilty of spending far too much time on social media. Facebook especially reels me in like a fish dangling from a hook. Losing all concept of time, I mindlessly flip through picture after picture, post after post.

If I'm honest, I can watch my mood spiral downward as time marches on. Fixing my attention on stories of protests, angry debates, and more and more people inciting hatred is anything but helpful to me. To be honest, I'm sick of it.

People share half-truths and pass along videos they don't realize have been edited and clipped to show only the story the media prefers to make known.

Blood boiling, I call on every ounce of self-control, desperately hoping to avoid fueling a fire. *Bite your lip, girl!*

The real issue is precious time that I'm wasting—time I can never recoup.

Girlfriend, let's take a step back. Instead of hours on our phones, let's consciously fill our minds with what we *know* to be true:

"Finally, brothers and sisters, whatever is true, whatever is noble, whatever is right, whatever is pure, whatever is lovely, whatever is admirable—if anything is excellent or praiseworthy—think about such things" (Phil. 4:8).

Listen, Sister: Purposefully open a Bible and read truth; it will refresh you. Let's remind ourselves and each other of who we really are. Then you will be filled with joy and confidence to move ahead with your purpose in mind: Love people. Share the good news.

Tossed by the Waves

e're blessed to live in Ontario. While winter is frigid and snowy and a solid number four on my list of favourite seasons, it takes up less than half the year. Eventually, summer shoulders her way in like a youngest child, fighting for her rightful turn.

Our city is nestled along the banks of Lake Huron, and a multitude of public beaches line the shores in our blue-water land. I love to wander barefoot along the sandy shoreline, exploring the beach for interesting shells, skipping stones, and driftwood, but my favourite find is always the beautiful beach glass.

I'm sure bystanders will tell you I resemble a one-toothed miner at a goldrush when I discover a piece of this colourful treasure and root around for more, digging through the shifting sand. Rolling the once-jagged edges of the silky, frosted prize in my hand, my mind wanders.

Wouldn't it be interesting to follow the life of this captivating piece of glass on the beach? Perhaps it began as a colourful bottle, an intended delivery on a freighter. Or maybe it was no longer needed and carelessly discarded by a passing boater. Better yet, maybe even it is part of a shipwreck that's secretly lurking just below the surface. Never would one imagine this piece of beauty would wash up on shore decades later.

A bottle floating then sinking deep below the surface as sand and sea enveloped her. Violent waves crashed, tossing her about in the fury of a storm. Bashing her against huge boulders, she shattered, chunks dispersing in all directions, impossible to reunite. Stirring, in pieces, she cycles with the water, buried and uncovered by the shifting sand. Drifting only at the will of the waves, the sea rejected her, spitting her up onto the beach amid rocks and shells. This peace was short-lived, lasting only until a new storm erupted and pelted the shore with savage waves, sweeping her back out to sea. And so it continued, beyond her control: sifting, tossing, moving. Finally she was thrust onto land, unrecognizable.

Have the storms of life ever swept you away? Have you, like me, tightly gripped the edge of your slippery, wet boat while wind and waves threatened to spill you headlong into the briny deep? Helpless, we're tossed and turned, thrown about in the ferocious surge as we crash headlong into a boulder.

The storm is intense, holding us captive in the grinding sand and pummeling us relentlessly, wearing us down. Like beach glass, our jagged edges are being softened, our rough surfaces smoothened as we're transformed into an unrecognizable treasure.

In this transformative process we find hope:

> "Consider it pure joy, my brothers and sisters, whenever you face trials of many kinds, because you know that the testing of your faith produces perseverance. Let perseverance finish its work so that you may be mature and complete, not lacking anything" (Jas. 1:2–4).

Listen, Sister: The calm, waveless days of still, blue water do nothing to perfect the glass. Without the storm, we would never change, never become the beautiful piece God designed. Thank Him today.

No Flossing Required

As my grown kids stand around, taunting each other and howling about the past, I invariably discover situations and adventures that happened years ago, right under my nose. I'm thankful that occasionally God allowed me a sliver of oblivion. I can't imagine adding the knowledge of one more day of shenanigans to that teetering young mom's consciousness. I much prefer hearing the stories now when I can laugh along with the crazy band of brothers and know they all survived and came out close friends at the other end.

It must have been twenty years ago because *Tarzan* had just been released on VHS. Young ones, this was pre-entertainment-on-demand, and returning home with the latest Disney movie in hand was a huge "mom win." The boys were thrilled.

With the promise of movie time in their future, I left the brothers to tidy up the basement. Apparently, the following is what transpired.

Reportedly, the cleaning assignment was going just fine until Cam, the youngest brother, did something ultra-annoying. According to Cam, his simple existence was enough to warrant harsh treatment from the others on any given day.

Grabbing dental floss from the bathroom drawer, the older two secured the annoying one to a wooden bunkbed post. Around and around, they pulled the floss and tightly knotted the end. By the sounds of it, they may have used the entire roll, the disappearance of which should have puzzled me since children are no fan of flossing.

As if restraining their brother was not punishment enough, they left the room to implement stage two of their little torture-fest.

Just beyond the bedroom door and out of sight, but well within earshot, the nasty boys began to chatter theatrically about the incredible *Tarzan* flick. In an improv production I'd love to see now, they commentated the storyline, hooting and hollering as they pretended to enjoy the movie without him.

While the brothers relentlessly teased and tormented Cam, he wrestled against the impenetrable floss, unable to break free. Although his anger raged and he fought with all his might, he was powerless to destroy the ties that bound him.

I had no idea this was happening at the time, and I'm still not sure how he got free. But I saw him yesterday, and I can report he is footloose and fancy-free all these years later.

Girlfriend, I have never been tied to a post with wire, but my heart has felt restrained as I desperately longed for freedom. Like a prisoner of my past, I trudged through life unable to remove the shackles of shame.

I knew Jesus, but I was missing the sense of peace I heard in the voice of other Christians. I could sense I was missing something, but lies from the enemy ambushed me and held me tightly trapped: *You'll never be good enough. Someone like you can never measure up. You're not like them. There's no use. Struggle is futile. Stay still, settle in.*

But Jesus came, and He set me free. He cut the ties that bound me up and reminded me that I am forgiven. He replaced the lies in my head with truth from His Word.

I am forgiven.

I am free.

I am a new creation.

I am loved.
I am His daughter.
John 8:36 says,

"So if the Son sets you free, you will be free indeed."

Jesus came and lived a perfect life, and they killed Him for it. Sister, He gave up His life once and for all to pay the price of your wrongs. Once we accept this gift from Him, this payment He made for us, we are forever free of our debt. He remembers our sin no more.

Oh, we still struggle. Sometimes I grab the dental floss and twirl in a tight spiral, strapping myself to the bedpost, forgetting that I've been set free. I listen to the lies of the accuser, reminding me of the girl I used to be. But God says I am His new creation. Those are words of life from His Word. So, let me remind you and myself at the same time: We have been bought at a high price. It is for freedom that we have been set free. No flossing required.

Listen, Sister: Are you all tied up inside today? Do you feel like you can never get it together? Is the past controlling you, binding you tight? You can be free! And freedom has a name: Jesus. What ties can you ask Jesus to cut today?

The Drive

I've been a mom for quite a while, and I've been a daughter even longer. I deliberately strive to instill wisdom in my children every chance I get, but I've come to realize that some of the biggest lessons we teach our kids are unintentional.

For example, my dad was a hoot. He loved playing games with us and instilled a lifelong passion for tabletop competition deep in my heart. I discovered that sitting around together playing board games made conversation easy, even if your goal was to annihilate your brother. I'm thankful for these opportunities to connect with my own growing family even now.

When my brothers and I were young, Dad had us play the "hold the bag game." He'd shovel a mixture of crushed corn and molasses into limp feed sacks while our wee hands gripped the soft, worn burlap, each of us impatiently waiting our turn in holding the bag steady. Everyone had a guess at how many shovels full it would take to fill the bag. Miraculously, we each had a turn at being right; even my baby brother, Greg, and he was a terrible guesser.

Like any good father, my dad was a teacher. Most of these lessons I didn't see as a child, and many I appreciate much more now that I'm grown. Do kids ever appreciate their parents' wisdom at the time?

My dad taught me the importance of the little things:

- Stop to really look at the roses.
- Never pass a lemonade stand without contributing.
- There is always time for a game.

But one of the most significant things he taught me came at an exceptionally dark time in my life. My marriage was crumbling. I was powerless, watching as the future I had envisioned vaporized before my eyes. As we often did, Dad and I went for a drive.

Pain poured down my face, with anguish, fear, disbelief, and endless heartache streaming hot. He drove. I bawled. He said not a word. Miles and miles from home, I was depleted and exhausted. Silence filled the air.

My dad shifted the car into park and turned in his seat to stare straight into my swelled eyes.

"Tess, I'm so sorry." And he cried.

My dad cried with me. And this is how it is with our heavenly Father.

When we empty our hearts to Him—our sadness, our fear, all of it—we can let it go. In fact, we are commanded to surrender it all to His capable hands:

"Cast all your anxiety on him because he cares for you" (1 Pet. 5:7).

He, as promised, always listens and, in return, replaces everything we handed Him with his perfect peace.

This is our good, good Father.

Listen, Sister: God always listens with compassion. He feels your pain, and He cares. Wow. The God of the universe cares for me and for you. I'm so thankful for this.

Finally Chosen

"**R**ed rover, red rover, we call Cindy over."

Do you remember this schoolyard game? Admitting so will be sure to expose your age. Apparently, it's been quite some time since schools have allowed such dangerous activities as charging with reckless abandon toward a haphazard chain of primary school friends.

In Red Rover, two teams line up, facing each other in an open field. Girls and boys of all shapes and sizes link arms, an impenetrable barrier. Or so they hope.

Carefully, teammates scrutinize their opponents. Eyes lock as weight, muscle, and speed are accessed from afar. Only the least threatening challenger will be selected.

Children wait with hopeful hearts. Please, please, please let it be me! Finally, the team captain (likely the largest and, therefore, toughest boy) calls me over. My heart swells. He called my name! I can barely believe it's true. I've been chosen. It doesn't matter one bit that it was for all the wrong reasons.

My heart flits with joy as my gangly legs trot towards the rival team. Carefully I choose the most promising juncture and thrust my way through tiny hands, hoping to tear apart the weakest link.

If I'm successful, I return a hero to my team and bring a captive opponent to beef up our forces. But most likely, I'll bounce back unsuccessful and meld into the rival squad, boosting their ranks.

Either way, I really don't care. They chose me. My name was called.

Don't we all want to be chosen? To hear the sound of our name ring out? God wove that very desire into our hearts when He created us, the desire to be selected, to be picked.

The Bible says God chose me to be His. If you're in a relationship with Jesus, He chose you too.

The knowledge that we're handpicked by God Himself is enough. We no longer need to just hope to be chosen.

Most of my life, I flitted from relationship to relationship, person to person, deeply craving acceptance. Like a puppy at the pound, I was hoping for love.

I was lost in a perpetual cycle, continually longing to be prized. And all along, God had already chosen me.

Truth is, I still struggle with this. I wonder if I always will. But here's what I've learned to be true: He is enough. We can be secure in His love. We don't need to beg for scraps from others or bait them and hope for the right answer to confirm our worthiness.

Countless times, I have set people up as the centre of my life. And countless times I have been let down by their inability to meet my needs physically, emotionally, and spiritually.

Do you ever find yourself in this place, hoping to be chosen and placing impossible expectations on the ones who love you? In reality, God has already given us all we need:

"Praise be to the God and Father of our Lord Jesus Christ, who has blessed us in the heavenly realms with every spiritual blessing in Christ. For he chose us in him before the creation of the world to be holy and blameless in his sight" (Eph. 1:3–4).

Listen, Sister: Take a collective step back and give God His rightful place in the heart of your life. He will never disappoint you. After all, He chose us first.

Wake Up, Sleeper

The children had been asleep for hours, and we were standing around the kitchen discussing politics, theology, or, more likely, which board game to play that evening. It's no secret that uninterrupted conversations are treasured by parents of small children.

I ignored it at first, but soon there was no mistaking the pitter-patter of little feet traipsing down the staircase. Paying no attention to those of us in authority, the blue-eyed tyke marched silently into the room and, without a word, made a beeline for the refrigerator. Using unprecedented strength, he swiftly yanked the fridge door open. Next, reaching down, he slid out the vegetable crisper and, in one swift motion, pulled down his pyjama pants and peed right into the crisper drawer.

The boy's eyes stared wide, and his face registered no knowledge of his mistake, only sweet relief. Later, he did not remember this, and to this day, I'm sure he will deny it.

Sleepwalking is a strange phenomenon. The person appears awake, but in a very real way, they're not.

Listen, Sister, a lot of us are sleepwalking through life. If I'm honest, I will admit it happens to me. Not this type of unfortunate fridge incident (that I remember) but there is no shortage of other examples. Have you ever grabbed your phone to check something quickly and been sucked into the space-time vortex? Have you picked up your cell to send a quick text and been trapped in the escape room of social media, needing to click every box before you set the phone down, wasting precious time? I'm guilty of this very thing.

The average American (and we Canadians are no different) checks his cell phone more than one hundred and fifty times a day and spends four and a half hours engaged on the little device in his pocket. *Four and a half hours.* These same people have also been heard saying things like, "I wish I had more time." Are we on to something here?

Have you seen people sleepwalking through life, missing the beauty of nature, the excited voices of their children, or the scent of freshly cut grass?

It's the world we live in, Girlfriend. My question to you is this: what are we missing? We have the appearance of being awake; our eyes are wide open, but are we really there? Are we spending more time engaging real people or engaging a cell phone?

As women, we have the corner on multi-tasking. Often, I think I can listen to someone in the room at the same time as I return a text message or check my notifications. I may try to look interested, nodding my head and murmuring, while staring at the device in my hand. Note, this is not an effective strategy. Being on the receiving end of this process can make the other person feel unimportant, like there's a contest for my attention and they lost. The winner is my cellphone. How sad is that?

Knowing we have one short life to live, let's spend it being engaged with real people. Let's spend it enjoying the world around us. Let's not sleepwalk through this life:

"But friends, you're not in the dark, so how could you be taken off guard by any of this? You're sons of Light, daughters of Day. We live under wide-open skies and know where we stand. So let's not sleepwalk through life like those others. Let's keep our eyes open and be smart. People sleep at night and get drunk at night.

But not us! Since we're creatures of Day, let's act like it. Walk out into the daylight sober, dressed up in faith, love, and the hope of salvation" (1 Thess. 5:4–8, MSG).

Listen, Sister: There is an enemy, and distraction is his game. If you're sent here by God to make a difference in this world—and you are—yet you spend life escaping reality, what's the cost?

Reminded

hat if I told you that my grandmother was the original Pinterest princess and her one-of-a-kind creations speak truth to us even today?

Grama was a bit of a collector. Her quaint war-time home was stuffed to the brim with knick-knacks, hand-starched doilies, and row upon row of African violets. As the summer breeze whispered warm through her kitchen window, the melody of tingly glass wind chimes danced in the air.

Growing up, I often lacked confidence. My insecurity seemed set in stone by unfortunate episodes, like wearing my dress tucked in my undies, falling up the stairs, and enduring other disastrous examples of typical childhood clumsiness. Instead of being protected and nurtured, I was ridiculed and teased, and years later, I still can't seem to forget.

But at Grama's house, it was different. We spent the days outside, watering flowers, visiting friends, and having tea. Suprisingly, she seemed to actually enjoy spending time with me. Come evening, she would "skootch over" in the rocking chair to make room for my bony butt, and I can't think of a single place I've felt more loved.

Her décor was eclectic, to say the least. Every wall was adorned with the most original hand-crafted signs, designed by none other than the spunky lady herself. She painstakingly snipped consonants and vowels out of piles of old magazines and glued them with glitter and yarn onto Styrofoam deli meat trays. She was also the princess of recycling.

As I describe them, I suppose these plaques were a bit odd, even back in the day. But for me, the truth contained within them returns to my mind years later. Pinterest move over; Dorothy is coming through. Here are a few of Grama's signs:

- For by grace are ye saved, through faith.
- Some folks miss heaven by twelve inches—the difference between head knowledge and heart belief.
- Love the Lord with all your heart, all your soul, and all your mind.

I wish I could go back there today, back to the carefree life of a little girl, back to the feeling of being treasured, cared for, and loved. And even as I consider this, I'm reminded that I really am all of these things. You are all of these things. We are God's treasure. He chose us. He cherishes us and loves us:

"The Lord your God is with you, the Mighty Warrior who saves. He will take great delight in you; in his love he will no longer rebuke you, but will rejoice over you with singing" (Zeph. 3:17).

I could really use a reminder these days. Could you? We all need to have signs, reminders to fill our heads with God's truth, like wall plaques, recipe cards, notes on the mirror.

Listen, Sister: Make His Word visible throughout the day so you can read it and soak it in. You need reminders of your true identity, a daughter of the King.
Styrofoam trays are optional.

Cold as Ice

It was late November and Cam's birthday. Most years this kid got ripped off by way of birthday celebrations, mainly because of his careless choice of birth dates. Because he arrived a few weeks before Christmas, each year I ended up trying to squeeze a party between holiday baking, decorating, and organizing gift lists for a bazillion kids. Add that to basic survival in an overflowing family of rowdy children hopped up on sugar and counting down the days until the jolly man in red made his appearance.

And don't think this mom didn't use Santa Claus as a threat for good behaviour. No judgment, Girlfriend, those were desperate times.

So, this must have been one of the rare years that Cam had a party, and I have pictures to prove it. After a gourmet meal of hotdogs and cake, we kicked the kids outside to clean up the aftermath. Suddenly, a startling crash filled the air, followed by the aftershock of glass splinters tingling. Racing to the rec room, the damage could not be missed.

The dilapidated mini blind bashed against the window frame as wind and snow rushed in through the shattered window. Shards of glass littered the floor, encircling a snowy ball of ice, roughly the size of a young boy's hand. Frustrated, I glanced over at my husband. It had been a long day, indeed.

It was not difficult to figure out where the ice ball had come from; I can still see the look on the small boy's face. He peered in the window, surveyed the devastating mess, and then locked eyes with me. And he bolted. I can't say where he went or what he thought, but by the time we finished the clean-up, he was back.

Apologizing, he explained that he thought the ball was soft snow when in fact it was a solid chunk of ice. The difference is indisputable; his crime was unintentional.

Girlfriend, have you ever inadvertently hurt someone? Have you ever spoken words before you took the time to filter them through your brain? I continually struggle with this very thing. We think we're tossing a fluffy ball of snow, but unknowingly, we whip a hunk of solid ice straight for a sweet friend's window.

At times, my misstep creates an awkward story to make my family cringe and provide laughter in the future. Other times, my thoughtless words shatter the glass and unintentionally hurl pain on some unsuspecting soul.

This week I was reminded of the anguish of childlessness. An aunt shared with me her pain, enduring thoughtless questions and insensitive comments for years. Perhaps not one person had intended to heap loads of agony on her tender heart. But they did. Lord, have mercy. Perhaps these are the instances Paul had in mind when he wrote,

"Let your conversation be always full of grace, seasoned with salt, so that you may know how to answer everyone" (Col. 4:6).

Listen, Sister: Be ever aware of this, and determine to carefully inspect your words before they leave your mouth (or keyboard) and determine their weight. Are they fluffy, light snow or rock-solid ice?

Chivaree

Have you ever heard of a *chivaree*? It's a hilarious, age-old redneck marriage custom that, sadly, seems to have died out over the years. I've got a good mind to resurrect it, but none of my unmarried kids seem to like the idea.

A few weeks after the wedding, a large group of friends and family gather again to pay a surprise visit to the happy couple. This usually happens late in the night and after the rowdy gang has been into the sauce for a bit.

The newlyweds are shocked awake by the deafening scream of a chain saw roaring directly below their bedroom. The uninvited entourage parades, hootin' and hollerin', into the humble abode at the first crack in the front door, making themselves comfortable as the blushing bride panics.

The night of tomfoolery includes such fun as hiding all the silverware, relocating the dining set to the roof, Jell-O in the bathtub, and, my personal favourite, removing labels from all the cans.

Shortly after my wedding, my always supportive brother Jake offered to babysit my house. You know, to make sure nothing terrible happened while we were out of town. How kind.

We returned home to a few practical jokes and vowed retribution if ever he could find a girl adventurous enough to agree to marry him. The odds were low.

But it wasn't until many weeks later the most surprising discoveries were made. I was annoyed to find my saltshaker full of sugar and even more bummed out to inadvertently add tabasco to my butter tarts. But the greatest shock came when the wrong label on cornstarch resulted in a hearty pot of beef stew exploding all over my kitchen.

Scrubbing meat and vegetables from your ceiling does nothing to quell anger.

The truth is, we all sport labels of some kind, and the wrong labels can really mess us up inside. When I'm tempted to toss the laptop through the front window after I've repeatedly forgotten the password, I call myself dumb. When I'm so tired I can't seem to put one foot in front of the other after nine o'clock at night, I label myself old and worn out. When I compare myself to the pretty girls who seem to have it all together—well, you get the idea.

Other people inadvertently assign us labels as well. Our friends, our co-workers, and even our parents negatively tag us, and these descriptors can stick:

- Uneducated
- Disorganized
- Failure
- Lazy
- Blabbermouth

We even stick labels on our own chests from time to time, and often these labels are hurtful and destructive:

- Divorced
- Rejected
- Loser

- Unloved
- Stupid

Girlfriend, here's the thing. Only the manufacturer knows what's actually inside. Only our Creator gets to say who we are. When we let these inaccurate labels define us, we're in for a heap of trouble.

All false labels come straight from the father of lies. He's sneaky and unscrupulous as he whispers them to our brains. But listen, Sister, he doesn't get to say who we are.

And there's more good news. We *can* combat those false descriptors and live in our true identity. Here are the five easy steps I've been working on these days:

- Pay careful attention to your thoughts. Stop and notice when you hear yourself think: "I am so _____."
- Compare that thought to *truth*. Ask yourself, *Is this what God says about me?*
- Squash the lie. Audibly say, "That is *not true*." People may stare at you when happens in public. Personally, I pretend I'm wearing air pods and fake a phone conversation. Avert your gaze and point to your ear if it gets too awkward.
- Envision ripping off that lie label and tearing it into teeny tiny pieces, denying it the chance to condemn you any longer.
- Cover yourself in *truth*. Stick the truth label right over where the lie label used to be. Use Gorilla Glue.

And what does God say our labels should be? Here are a few ways God describes the people who love and follow Him:

- Complete
- Capable
- Welcomed by God

- Treasured
- Dearly loved

With these correct labels firmly fixed, we are off and running to do what we were intended to do. Pray this verse when you feel the lie labels threatening a comeback:

"Therefore, as God's chosen people, holy and dearly loved, clothe yourselves with compassion, kindness, humility, gentleness and patience" (Col. 3:12).

Listen, Sister: Let's pay careful attention. Listen to your thoughts. Scrutinize your labels and make sure they're an accurate match for who your Creator says you are.

Morning Comes Early

I woke with a start an hour before my alarm, continuing the exhausting pattern beyond my control. Sleep had become as elusive as that perfect match on any online dating site. And even with all those hours lying awake, my brain fully engaged, it was days before I would learn the reason why.

I'd lived through several sleep stages of life already. The "tired teenager" stage, sleeping as long as possible until Dad kicked my butt out of bed; the "exhausted mom of infants" stage where breastfeeding nominated me for every middle-of-the-night party time; the bad dreams and anxiety of the "middle school worries" stage; and rounding it out, the "teenager has my car" delayed sleep routine.

Finally, I'm at the long-desired stage where, theoretically, I can sleep through the night. It's been a long time coming, Sister. So, as I lay in my bed, awake too early for several days straight, I was less than excited to see the clock glaring back at me with the same premature number.

Turning my pillow over, I rooted for the cool side. *Is caffeine the culprit?* I wondered. I'd been avoiding all such things after dinner since this insomnia marathon began. No coffee, no tea, no Coke, and essentially no chocolate (well, maybe a slim, almost transparent sliver that was basically invisible).

Tossing and turning, I rolled onto my back and folded my legs, tenting the duvet, and listened to my husband softly breathe, oblivious to my frustration. Slithering down in the bed and rolling onto my tummy, I tucked my feet over the edge of the mattress, the cool, smooth footboard against the soles of my feet.

Desperate for sleep to visit my racing brain, I prayed. I thanked God for a boundless list of blessings, purposefully making no mention of the gift of menopause. Wide awake, praying turned to thinking through my list of family and friends, and I remembered a Bible study that I was invited to join. I wanted to learn more, and the study looked interesting, but I didn't have that kind of time in my day. I silently prayed, "Lord, please give me time to join this study, to be in your Word—just an extra hour a day."

Bam! It hit me like a ton of bricks. All week I had been asking God for more time, and He had been giving it to me, one hour every day.

Listen, Sister, how often are we asking God for the very things He is already giving us? He wants us to bring our requests to Him with thanksgiving, to tell Him what we need, and He also promises to provide all of it. He deeply desires for us to be in relationship with Him, to be tuned in, listening and watching for opportunities.

Imagine your son asking for something he needs. Because you love him and want to give him good things, you gladly place it directly in front of him. But imagine that instead of noticing, he continues to flip flop around, asking you to give it to him over and over. Thankfully, God is abundantly more patient than I am as a parent.

Over the years, I've heard other Christians talk about hearing God, and I didn't really get it. No loud voice ever boomed from above, and no legible writing appeared on the wall of my bedroom. So, I felt like I was a substandard Christian. But I've learned the process of spiritual growth takes time and intentionality. God speaks through the Bible, our thoughts, and the wise words of mature believers. As we grow in relationship with God, we learn to recognize how He communicates with us. He invites us all to the conversation:

"Call to me and I will answer you and tell you great and unsearchable things you do not know" (Jer. 33:3).

Listen, Sister: I'm so thankful that God is a master communicator. Let's learn not just to talk to God but also to listen for Him as the Holy Spirit makes us aware.

That's Uncomfortable

S pending a week at the cottage was the highlight of the summer for our rambunctious tribe. The boys messed around for hours on their own, searching for minnows and jumping off the dock into the cool, refreshing waters of a northern Ontario lake. S'mores around a roaring campfire always rounded out the day as we swatted mosquitoes and stock-piled memories to last a lifetime.

Our middle group of sons included five boys in the span of four years. Although they were bumper to bumper in age, there was a well-established, unspoken rule among the brothers of who bossed who, who avoided who, and who temporarily held the power. This pecking order could be challenged at a moment's notice on the kitchen floor, with witnesses.

But there was something about vacation that suspended the normal sibling hierarchy. Each year, the cottage provided an unofficial "time out," a temporary hiatus among all the siblings. They could hang out together treating each other well, like decent human beings, all day long with no lasting culpability.

They horsed around outside from sunup to sundown, with rainy days offering countless rounds of chess and spoons and comic books galore.

Keeping the cottage tidy was always a challenge. We had next to zero housekeeping rules that week, but I nearly lost my mind every single day, finding wet bathing suits in puddles of lake water on the bedroom floors. Ricky, more anxious for peace than worried about the real problem, came up with an ingenious plan that changed our cottage life forever. Any bathing suit found discarded on the floor in a wet heap was immediately chucked into the freezer.

Girlfriend, I have to tell you, I felt some deep satisfaction when it came time to swim. Watching each careless kid crack the frozen leg holes open to pry his little feet into the colourful block of ice was a moment to cherish.

The boys caught on relatively quickly. They were never hurt, but it sure wasn't comfortable wearing that frozen swimsuit. And that, my friend, is how they remembered; in the discomfort, they learned to pause and consider their actions.

Similarly, when my life is just buzzing along, tickety-boo, and I'm content and comfortable, I'm likely to quietly and confidently keep moving in the same manner. But at other times, when God nudges me into an uncomfortable place, my gut response is to bolt. *No, no, no, no . . . Fix this! Change this! Bring back my soft blankie!*

Listen, Sister, are you like me? Do you love comfort and hate pain? Good! You are indeed a human being.

It seems counter-intuitive, but I'm learning it's actually OK to sit in the discomfort, to spend quiet time with God listening and being thankful. The discomfort compels us to read His Word over and over again, scrawling words with trembling fingers and blurry eyes. We cry out to Him in hot tears as acid burns a crater in the pit of our chest.

My friend, He hears every word and holds every tear. This is not easy. This is brutal. And this is life changing. The psalmist wrote,

"You have seen me tossing and turning through the night. You have collected all my tears and preserved them in your bottle! You have recorded every one in your book" (Ps. 56:8, TLB).

Listen, Sister: Often, it's in the uncomfortable that we are changed. And it's OK to sit in it because we never sit alone.

Time Flies

The MGM lion roars as the audience settles into their seats. The buzz of excitement is soon overpowered by the thundering film score. In gigantic, bold letters the movie title unfolds: *A Year in the Life of Tess Scott.*

My chest burns hot. My mind reels. The thought of my life on the big screen for all to see is terrifying: *Who plays me? What about all of the terribly awkward things I seem to continually do? Morning hair?*

I can't think of a single movie-worthy event in my life these days. I have lots of dreams, goals, and ideas I intend to get around to, but I just haven't had time.

Have you ever said—or heard it said if you're under thirty—"There's not enough hours in the day"?

I wonder how many hours would be enough for us: twenty-five, twenty-six? If we had five additional hours a day, would we devote them solely to important, life-changing events?

And while we're fleshing this out, which activities are important? Which are the essential actions we need to spend time on?

As Jesus Girls, I believe we are all "on mission." Now, that sounds like an exciting adventure movie, doesn't it? We're called to share the Good News. We're told to spend our lives loving other people.

Sometimes love looks like delivering meals or listening to a friend's bad day or explaining why we have joy and hope when it makes no sense in undeniably difficult circumstances.

But love comes at a cost. Maybe it costs money, but it always costs time. And we value time in our society, don't we? Sort of.

If someone asks for help on moving day, you may not have time. Read your Bible every morning? It's difficult to find the time. But I suspect every one of us has absentmindedly clicked on social media and been lured into a twisty-turny rabbit hole, oblivious to our surroundings, for minutes on end. Haven't we? Most of us carry around a mini life-suction machine, right in our own hands, draining away minutes over and over, day after day.

Studies show we tap, swipe, and click our phones 2,617 times in a twenty-four-hour period; the average cell phone user spends four hours and thirty-three minutes on their smartphones and tablets every single day (https://www.bankmycell.com/blog/smartphone-addiction/#chapter1). I suspect that number is growing each year, don't you? I found this even more shocking when the math girl in me realized this daily screen time adds up to over sixty-eight *days* a year. That's more than two of our twelve months sucked into an electronic device. Wowzers! Honestly, when I check my own screen time app, I am often surprised and frustrated at the score.

Girlfriend, we all start out with the same twenty-four hours in a day, though the number of our days is unknown. This is the thing about time: we can't make more; we can't put time on hold; and once it's gone, we can never get it back. Let's use it wisely.

Here are a few suggestions I'm preaching to myself lately:

- Be conscious of your time and live intentionally.
- List your goals for the day, the month, and the year and revisit this list often to stay accountable.
- Limit social media. Have a device-free day or even segment of time. Turn off notifications; avoid the rabbit hole.
- Ask God to open your eyes to see opportunities to love on people.

- Grow a courageous spirit. When you see an opportunity, do it.
- Live in the moment. Be present.

It's deflating to glance back over the day and witness myself running around like a chicken with its head cut off. Have you ever actually seen this? It's a bloody mess. Not only is the chicken flapping in circles, accomplishing no good thing, but she is also completely unaware of her predicament.

But by living life in step with the Holy Spirit, our story will be one of adventure, love, and deep purpose. The Old Testament prophet Micah describes living with such purpose:

"He has shown you, O mortal, what is good. And what does the Lord require of you? To act justly and to love mercy and to walk humbly with your God" (Mic. 6:8).

And that kind of life makes a movie I look forward to watching.

Listen, Sister: How are you filling your days? Ask God to open your eyes to opportunities to love on people.

Not a False Alarm

A few years ago, at exactly the time I was praising God for restoring our marriage from divorce—the most monumental miracle so far in my life—I was diagnosed with breast cancer. This announcement blindsided me, striking like an anvil plunging from a desert cliff above. I didn't see it coming. The next time, I would.

In hindsight, God's timing, including the timeline of this devastating diagnosis, was perfect. He healed my body and encouraged my heart, never leaving my side. He allowed my "new" husband to demonstrate his love for me in tangible ways. I witnessed God orchestrate friendships, rekindle relationships, and nourish my spirit through the time of surgery, chemotherapy, and radiation.

After a few years of ongoing battles with fear, body image, and identity, our married life settled into our new normal—or as normal as it gets for a lopsided chick with one boob.

So, I was shocked to receive a call from my surgeon asking to discuss the results of my most recent MRI. She offered an appointment the next day and suggested I bring my husband. Sister, this is never good news.

The next twenty-four hours crept by as my mind spun through a bazillion scenarios. I did self-checks, consulted Google, and revisited dates of past examinations while an invisible drill pierced a hole through my chest into my heart. Anxiety drowned out any rational thoughts. I reminded myself to breathe.

My list of "what-ifs" compounded minute by minute, and each worry became truth in my mind. I planned out future conversations with each of my children, chose pallbearers, and wrote a note to my BFF regarding suitable casket attire. Sister, this kind of decision cannot be left to the men.

As morning finally dawned, I wrapped up my frantic list of things I had yet to do in life:

- Spend time with grandkids.
- Lie in a field looking up at the stars.
- Tell my story.
- Write a book.
- Learn to play the banjo.

Things that did not make the list:

- Eat less chocolate.
- Refrain from hugging.
- Spend time alone.
- Watch more Netflix.

Finally, the appointed time arrived, and the doctor delivered the news. I was fine. The surgeon was simply closing my file and sending me back to my family doctor, who would monitor my health and test for cancer yearly. Simultaneously, Ricky and I let out an enormous sigh of relief.

It was a false alarm. But, Girlfriend, what if it was, in fact, meant to be a real alarm? What if it was a call to wake me up and remind me to smell the roses? Perhaps it was an enormous nudge to pursue my calling and appreciate life. The psalmist realized how easily we take life for granted and prayed,

"Show me, Lord, my life's end and the number of my days; let me know how fleeting my life is. You have made my days a mere handbreadth; the span of my years is as nothing before you. Everyone is but a breath, even those who seem secure" (Ps. 39:4–5).

Listen, Sister: The number of days God has given you on this earth doesn't change; it is finite. We're in a countdown, and one day, it will be my last and yours. Isn't that a strange thought? So, as long as you have time left, consider it, enjoy it, and do not waste a single day.

Restrained

As I mentioned earlier, I'm at the parenting stage now where my kids feel safe to reveal some childhood shenanigans of which I was unaware.

Recently, I was privy to a conversation among the brothers about a practical joke that took place some twenty years ago. Tremendous laughter ensued with all but one son excited to recount the story.

Back in those days, dinner was a real freak show. The chaos of ravenous children rough-housing and the promise of some sort of food to fill their bellies made for a noisy gathering. Let me tell you, there were no fancy four-course meals, and thankfully posting a picture of your dinner on social media wasn't yet invented.

A seat was empty at the table, and when asked, the brothers were quick to report that Cam was eating at a friend's. This warranted no further investigation. I knew the friend, and frankly, as a mom of small kids, I was just fighting to get through the day.

Recently, amid this joking at Cam's expense, I discovered he was, in fact, home that day. Well, he was on the property. While they relaxed together, devouring every last crumb, their younger brother was in the backyard duct taped to a lawn chair.

What? Noooooooooo!

Restrained and helpless, he couldn't move a muscle. His pitiful cries went unheard, and not a soul rushed to his aid. It wasn't fair. It made no sense. That young lad, frustrated and starving, was missing out. Discouraged, his mind searched, wondering why his mom—protector, nurturer, and chief cook—would not answer his pleas for help.

Have you ever felt like life is not fair? You might have felt powerless, excluded, and abandoned, like a spectator watching from the sidelines as others went about their wonderful lives.

I've been there, too, in both overwhelming and significant things and also in less tragic but equally puzzling daily occurrences. So, what do we know to be true?

We know that feelings are *not* truth.

Nobody said life would be fair. As a matter of fact, God says quite the opposite. We will have trouble in this world, but we can have peace.

And we know that God Himself hears our cries. He never leaves us in the hard. He is the God of compassion. He hears our cries and comes to our aid.

Often life doesn't make sense to us in the moment. I can see only the present and remember a small part of the past. But God is not restricted by time. He is in the past, present, and future and fully understands all things.

I believe that the Creator of the universe has the power to rescue you and me. He promises this. We can trust Him. Consider John 16:33:

"I have told you these things, so that in me you may have peace. In this world you will have trouble. But take heart! I have overcome the world."

And even though He is all-powerful, He desires a relationship with us. Doesn't that just blow your mind? It does mine. And that is the kind of truth that I choose to remember.

Listen, Sister: Are you struggling with a difficult situation today that doesn't make sense? Our God hears you. Trust Him today.

The Hair Clip

I'm a morning person and somewhat OCD, which means I can get a pile of stuff done before seven o'clock. Unfortunately, any deviation from my scheduled plan and fasten your seatbelts; we're all going somewhere hot in a handbasket. This was one of those mornings.

My teenage son's current obsession was his hair. His "friend-girl" had just completed a five-day marathon of nightly braiding his wet strands into tiny rows so that each morning he would wake to a head full of strawberry blonde curls—an ambitious and non-sustainable plan.

I run a tight ship in the morning without a minute to spare, so just before I set out to blow dry my own hair, I popped into the kitchen to refill my mug. (Thank you, sweet Jesus, for hot coffee in the morning.)

With blow-dryer in hand, I reached into the bathroom drawer for my hair clip. The hair clip was not there. Now, unless you have frustratingly short hair (and God did not bless you with the talent of all things "girl" – also related to why He did bless me with an army of all sons, such a wise God), you may not understand the importance of the simple hair clip in the complicated blow-drying process. It's vital. I checked the next drawer, no clip. I looked in the cupboard, no clip. An overwhelming feeling of panic filled my senses, and my chest constricted just a little. I did not have time for this. I thought back, desperately searching my mind for where the clip could be.

"Hayden!" Obviously, this was his fault. He was always borrowing my stuff, and I could find anything from Tupperware bowls to my "borrowed" slippers in his bedroom at any given time. I burst through his door with the urgency of a mother of five rushing for a bathroom with a sneeze coming on.

"Hayden! Where is my hair clip? . . . Yes, I know it's six o'clock . . . Yes, I know your alarm is set for seven."

I was certain he must have used it in last night's braiding extravaganza. Sleepily and barely audibly, he denied any knowledge of my claim.

Another frantic sweep of the bathroom ensued but yielded no clip. I searched the kitchen counters, drawers, and fridge. Yes, I searched the fridge. I have done a few dumb things, so this location was not out of the question. No hair clip was found. Oh. My. Word.

I might have to call in sick. I did not have this kind of time to waste in the morning. Then I remembered the family room. Aha! I scoured the area where the braiding activity took place. No luck. I did another scan of the boy's bedroom, but this time I used my less invasive, handy cell phone flashlight and didn't wake him up (because I'm not a crazy woman). No hair clip was located.

By now, panic had full reign in my mind, and I was beginning to reel out of control. I called my husband at work. Yes, he is a first responder and generally busy on the job. But this *was* an emergency. As it turned out, he had not seen my hair clip and did not share my sense of urgency.

I was dangerously close to the "no turnaround" point in my morning schedule. I considered whether "hair malfunction" might be approved on a sick-day request. Many precious moments had been wasted searching like a madwoman, and I had no choice but to try to salvage what I could from my mostly air-dried head of hair.

As I grabbed my hairbrush and looked with full-on dread into the bathroom mirror, I spotted it, the hair clip. It was in my hair the entire time.

Have you ever had days like this when everything feels like it is spinning out of control? Life seems crazy, and there is barely time to breathe between the kids, the house, and dumping another basket of laundry onto the couch to be folded. Days are a blur of runny noses, homework sheets, chauffeur duties, and incessant whining. And food. Every single day they want to eat! It's too much.

And you wonder about and maybe even compare yourself to those other moms with their perfectly blow-dried hair. In your mind's eye, you can see them sitting at their cleared-off kitchen tables, reading an inspiring devotional while they sip chai and their children (wearing adorable, clean outfits) play together for hours quietly in the next room.

Do you know what these women are? Imaginary!

Girlfriend, give yourself some grace so you can give that grace to the rest of us too. Eventually, we can all bask in it, in acceptance and grace:

"Therefore encourage one another and build each other up, just as in fact you are doing" (1 Thess. 5:11).

Listen, Sister: Give yourself a break. We're all just making it through one day at a time. And trust me, this stage of life you're at, it won't last forever. It will feel like it, though. And then, one day, it won't. And you'll look around and see you've survived. And then it will be your chance to encourage another mama to hang in there.
And every once in a while, remember to look in the mirror.

Talent Show

I 've never been particularly talented at any one thing. I've noticed lots of people seem to have a natural inclination toward a sport or a special ability that makes its appearance early in childhood. But not me. After fifty years, I was ready to throw the towel in, but finally, in the nick of time, I may have discovered something important.

When my brother Jack and I were youngsters, our parents enrolled us in piano lessons. I was not "a natural," but I did learn to read music and respect the value of practice, which I avoided continually. God bless Mrs. Fuller, who showered grace and kindness on both of us back in the day.

Our extended family is jam-packed with lively, entertaining people. All anniversaries, weddings, or celebrations of any kind have required a sizable venue. I have thirty-five first cousins on my dad's side; we're no small potatoes, Girlfriend. The rented hall usually featured a stage, and that's all the encouragement this rowdy crowd needed.

Aunts and uncles lined up to step dance, recite poems, sing ditties, and perform skits. Jake the Peg, the three-legged crooner, was always a crowd favourite. Our family overflows with talent.

I've never had a problem pointing out distinct gifts in any of our eight sons either. That's a no-brainer. Our family tree is ripe with talented people.

But I've never seen myself as one of them. Instead, I've stumbled around, feeling insecure in my own skin and yearning for some sort of special ability. Why can't I just do something meaningful?

Over the years, and seemingly unconnected to this great search for purpose, I sensed God nudging me to share my story—but not the kind of nudge your brother gives you when you're teetering beside the edge of the pool fully clothed. This was different.

It seemed everywhere I turned there were signs pushing and prodding, coaxing me along to write stories and encourage women. I felt very sure that this was from God, but at the same time, I was not a writer. I had no special ability, skill, or degree, but I did have about a bazillion reasons why I couldn't possibly do it. Still, He urged me forward.

I'd like to tell you that I obeyed immediately, like a lowly human interacting with almighty God. But that would be a lie. I argued, avoided, appealed, and suggested other women who better fit the position. I made a list of reasons why I was not the girl for the job. Highlights included my sordid past (who would listen to me?), my lack of education, and my steadily depleting confidence.

One by one, God took his giant permanent marker and stroked things off that list, teaching me that this is *His* story; I only play a small part. I'm discovering He will continually equip me for anything He asks me to do and then carry me precisely the distance He intends for me to go.

Listen, sister, I still get thrown off the track sometimes. We all do. I forget that this is His story and I get all balled up, worried about next steps and how in the world I can do any of it.

Does this sound familiar to you? Girlfriend, we need to ignore the lies in our heads and remember the One who called us is faithful. He will supply all we need to get the job done: the talent, the timing, and the tools. He will provide the ability and the opportunity to do His bidding. We only need to take the very next step:

"Commit to the Lord whatever you do, and he will establish your plans" (Prov. 16:3).

Listen, Sister: Are you panic-stricken at the thought of obeying God? Trust Him today for the next step forward.

Lavished in Love

A few years ago, we established the exciting tradition of allowing our grandkids to choose their own birthday gift. This idea has morphed into a day-long birthday extravaganza, including dinner at their favourite restaurant and the undivided attention of doting grandparents.

The highlight of this grand celebration, of course, is a trip to the toy store. Choosing the prize is always an interesting process as the decision-making is painstakingly slow and deliberate. The endless options are mind-boggling. One choice. Make it good.

Back in 2020, one birthday shopping spree (like a million other events) was severely delayed. Finally, the big day arrived, and our sweet girl took her turn shopping with Grandad.

In a world of tiny toys, Shopkins, and Beanie Babies, I was shocked at the sight of this little gal, vibrating with excitement as she strained to carry a ginormous stuffed unicorn.

Don't we just love to give our children wonderful presents? Our heavenly Father is like this. He loves to lavish us with amazing gifts.

To be honest, some days I'm just not feeling it. My life doesn't feel amazing. Whether it's raging hormones, the disappointment of canceled plans, or last year's T-shirts that shrank in winter storage (yes, this happens), my thoughts get me down.

My focus backfills my mind, so hear this: Where we focus—the things we read, scroll through, and listen to—fills our minds. Next, these thoughts affect our emotions and our mood.

With this in mind, I've been noticing the good: a ball of fire 93,000,000 miles away warming my skin; lyrics I needed to hear, at exactly the right moment, speaking directly to my heart; flowering Clematis clinging to indifferent fence boards; dragonflies noiselessly gliding, kissing the cool surface of the water.

Every morning, my brother and I text each other with three things we're thankful for: good sleep, bike rides, Steph's cookies. It's a wonderful way to start the day and helps me to find joy amid trouble. Because believe me, not every day is smooth sailing.

I challenge you to do this too. Try it this month. Every morning, before you check social media, before you get sidetracked with your overwhelming to-do list, take a moment. Jot down three things that you are thankful for. Join me as we embrace a life of gratitude and thank the One who takes joy in giving each of us our own giant unicorn:

> "So then, just as you received Christ Jesus as Lord, continue to live your lives in him, rooted and built up in him, strengthened in the faith as you were taught, and overflowing with thankfulness" (Col. 2:6–7).

Listen, Sister: You can *choose* to fill your mind with truth. Recognize and focus on the good gifts.

No Rest for the Weary

As the parent of a gang of small children, bedtime was my favourite time of day. Can I get an amen here?

I love my kids and all, but a home bustling with constant activity and never-ending excitement was downright exhausting. Life was hectic with schedules to coordinate, housekeeping chores, and constant calls to referee squabbles. By the end of the day, my legs, heavy with fatigue, were only encouraged up the stairs by the hope of a few precious hours of peace and quiet.

"The littles" at our house were, of course, the most work and not coincidentally assigned the earliest bedtime. Stories were short and sweet, and more than once my eyelids let me down, closing heavily, mid-sentence. So. Very. Tired.

I recall one endless day when the sun could not go down quickly enough. Cuddling my two little toe heads, I recited a familiar story for the zillionth time and clenched my teeth in an effort to stay awake.

Almost there. A few short minutes and I could collapse, dead weight, into my pillow in joyous relief.

"Don't forget to pee. Run along to the bathroom. Off you go," I reminded the little guys.

And then it happened. As close as I was to clutching my sweet rest, it was quickly ripped from my grasp.

In response, my sweet child said something that changed my evening plans in a way I never expected. "Mom, we don't need the bathroom," he explained, staring up between long lashes. "We just pee in the LEGO bin."

You what?

Surely this was some sort of silly joke.

Nope.

Evidently, these two small boys had, in fact, been peeing in the giant LEGO bin for quite some time. Removing the lid confirmed this fact in short order as the pungent odour enveloped the small bedroom instantly.

Instead of an evening of rest and relaxation, I faced a few hours of operational decisions, hard work, and reflection on my choice of motherhood as a primary career.

I don't remember what I said to the little darlings, but it was likely something profound and often spoken when subsequent generations of parents discover two thousand LEGO bricks swimming in a sea of urine.

All this to say, parenthood is not for sissies. It's draining, frustrating, and often overwhelming.

Bizarre circumstances will crop up again and again. There will be no guidelines or easy answers. And you may feel like you are alone in the craziness of motherhood. Oh, and you will be tired. (Did I mention that?) A bowl of cereal can be considered a healthy dinner, and wearing matching shoes is to be commended.

If you've graduated from the raising-little-kids stage of life, maybe you can pass on some encouragement to a mom who is trying to hang in there today. Here are a few things I wish I had known:

- Lower your expectations to avoid disappointment. This applies to all areas and every relationship.
- Short books still count as bedtime stories. You get no extra points for the number of pages read.
- Do what you can and don't feel guilty for what you can't.

- There are *no* perfect families or perfect homes. You just don't see the other side. We didn't have social media way back when, and I cannot imagine how hard it must be today to remind yourself that perfection is a lie. Online posts are often not the whole story.
- It's OK to accept help.

Even now, I struggle with my desire for perfection in certain areas of life. Girlfriend, it's good to have goals; no problem there. But when we fall short, when we're too busy to do all we want to do, or when the world around us isn't up to snuff, how can we hold it all together?

We can return to the source of our peace and rest:

"Come to me, all you who are weary and burdened, and I will give you rest. Take my yoke upon you and learn from me, for I am gentle and humble in heart, and you will find rest for your souls. For my yoke is easy and my burden is light" (Matt. 11:28-30).

Listen, Sister: Here's what I've been trying to learn. An important step, God's counter-intuitive directive, is rest. In the face of a world that pushes for more, more, more, take a step back. Live one day at a time and do the things you can. Don't get all tangled up in knots. Make this your new goal, to live at peace.

What Kind of Friend Are You?

I can barely stand to think back to that time. Maybe because my mind wishes to block the pain and pretend it didn't happen. But I force myself to work through it, hoping to prevent any such tragedy in the future for myself and perhaps for you.

As a woman, I tend to share secrets with the friend I know will be on my side. I gravitate toward the girl I am sure will be in my corner.

These days, I have a growing group of friends with all sorts of gifts and personalities. This was not the case back then. One by one, I moved away from anyone who didn't approve of my choices. I replaced true friends with some good-time girls who would never challenge my decisions. It was a black storm brewing, setting the stage for a terrible catastrophe. And terrible it was.

All these years later, I struggle to write these words without sobbing. God has been so very good to me. His forgiveness and the forgiveness of my family and friends are incredible gifts that I do not deserve. I have discovered God is willing, able, and pleased to redeem *absolutely everything* in anyone's life (including mine and yours) and turn it around for His glory and my good.

Hopefully, you have not been a "storm causer" in your life. But maybe you have. I'm here to tell you that no matter what you have done, there is forgiveness in Christ. He's not surprised by any of it, and He is waiting to hear from you, arms wide open.

To hopefully prevent further catastrophes, for myself and others, I want to share some guidelines I've learned about friendships:

- Seek out people who graciously speak truth into your life. Find friends who aren't afraid to take you to task if you are screwing up. We all need friends who will tell us the truth in loving, kind ways, even if it's hard.

- When you find that close friend, that person you can trust, the girl you just "click" with, tell her *everything*. *Note, the whole church prayer chain does not need to hear everything. The prayer request offered at small group does not need to include everything. But your BFF she needs to hear everything. Sometimes, we want to keep that last 2 percent hidden away. We think if she knew that sinful habit or thought, she might not love us the same way. But here's the truth, Sister. When we keep that secret hidden inside, it's like we give it more power. When we say it out loud, we crush it. So, ask for prayer. Ask for help. Oh, how I wish I had done this all those years ago.

- Be that true friend. Be genuine. Be real. Speak truth into the lives of your friends. You cannot sincerely love someone without giving them God's truth. And you can't give them truth without wrapping it in love. It's a delicate balance, and one you'll need to pray over continually.

- Pray for each other. Pray with each other. Pray in person. Pray on the phone. Pray together in the car, walking down the road, and sitting in the sunshine enjoying an iced tea.

These are things that I'm still learning, usually the hard way. Like most lessons in life, it takes time. But when our heartfelt and persistent prayers are promised to have tremendous power, how can we lose? James give us this assurance in his epistle:

"Therefore, confess your sins to one another [your false steps, your offences], and pray for one another, that you may be healed and restored. The heartfelt and persistent prayer of a righteous man [believer] can accomplish much [when put into action and made effective by God—it is dynamic and can have tremendous power]" (Jas. 5:16, AMP).

Listen, Sister: Who are your true friends? Can you tell them your hard truth?

That's So Not Neat

Does your awkward teenage self ever creep up on you? Do insecurity and doubt wrestle their way back into your brain all these years later? Just when I think I've finally left those feelings behind. Bam! Here I go again.

I didn't grow up with Nike's, lobster bisque, or Disney Cruise Line vacations. Sister, I'm a survivor of home perms, hand-me-down clothes, and camping in a homemade tin trailer on the reserve. We had everything we needed, but it was not a pretentious life, not by a long shot.

Years later, all my sons' wives are incredible women. Every one of them is delightful, kind, self-confident, and obviously patient. I'm over the moon, thankful to finally have daughters. And these girls have been nothing but gracious to me, so I've made every attempt to avoid embarrassing them in public. I mean, my boys are somewhat accustomed to it by now, but these girls are delicate flowers.

It was early summer, and the pool was finally open. The window for warm weather in Ontario is a very small one, lethargically opening and then springing closed again at a moment's notice. As a survival strategy, we Canadians learn to dress in layers. When the sun shows itself, we remove the winter garb, keeping it close just in case. I have worn shorts and fuzzy mittens in the same week on more than one occasion.

But once summer is here to stay, it's a non-stop frenzy of popsicles and hotdogs before the clouds roll in with snow once again.

We were lounging by the water, the first time in our bathing suits (also known as the base layer), waiting for our kids to arrive with the littles in tow. As I basked in the warm sun and breathed in the sweet lilacs, it suddenly became evident that I needed to take care of some "bathing suit bottom business." You know, things that aren't quite as important when you're clad nine months straight in long underwear and turtlenecks.

Horrified, I sprang from my chair and back into the house for an overdue appointment with a bottle of hair removal treatment. Dodged a bullet there, my friend. Waiting the four to six prescribed minutes, I let myself imagine the horror on my sweet girl's face had I unknowingly subjected her to that atrocity. Lord, have mercy.

Hearing the kids shouting their arrival, I rushed back out to the yard with a sigh of relief and a handful of popsicles. We watched the children swim and splash until, out of the corner of my eye and somewhere down near my knee, I spotted it: a nasty old gob of dark hair glued to my leg in plain sight. Have you ever held a conversation with someone, all the while trying not to look at something so they won't see it? Have you also tried to convince yourself that "the thing" does not exist and this episode is merely a throwback of another disturbing event in ninth grade?

The good news is that in my heart, I know that my daughters love me. They don't judge me for my embarrassing antics or think less of me for any part of who I am. The issue isn't them; the issue is me.

Our identity, who we really are, is decided by the One who made us. We need to keep these truths playing over and over in our minds: *I am uniquely and wonderfully made. I am chosen, loved, and cherished.*

As we continue to show grace to each other, we will live in freedom in our imperfect world, the freedom to be who we were meant to be. Some were created to walk a runway, and others were made to make women smile. Both can be part of God's perfect plan:

> "You saw me before I was born. Every day of my life was recorded in your book. Every moment was laid out before a single day had passed" (Ps. 139:16).

Listen, Sister: Search the Bible for five words God uses to describe you. Write them down and practice saying them out loud.

Isn't She Something?

The whir of the grinder and the aroma of freshly ground, dark-roasted coffee beans permeated the air as I skipped along the reflective floors in the beverage aisle at A&P. My grandfather slowed, allowing me to catch up; everything about his appearance was a stark contrast to mine. In this contrast lay my heartfelt security.

Grampa was a mountain of a man, strong as an ox, hard-working, and uncompromising in his convictions. His dull work shirt and worn-out pants seemed to illuminate my fresh, white leotards, plaid skirt, and clicky black shoes. The man was friendly, thoughtful, and loved me generously.

We visited the grocery store often, and without fail, Ivan, the hefty, bald butcher, would rush over to say hello. He doted over me, paying careful attention to how much I had grown since our last visit (which was, without exception, a lot).

But each time I spied him making his way to me, a sharp spring clamped inside my chest and wound painfully tighter as he approached. Ivan was a kind man, but I felt anxious and fearful because, well, big bald guys are scary to wee, little girls.

Grampa would hold my quivering hand tightly in his and declare, "Isn't she something?"

This was old folks' talk for, "See her? She's mine. I'm so proud of this girl."

I was young, defenseless, and terrified, but he was mighty, strong, and fearless. As I held on to him, my panic subsided.

Because of my Grampa's great love for me, I felt safe and at peace. I knew he loved me because he told me, and he showed me. He announced to the world I was his grandchild and lavished me with tender words, hugs, and pumpernickel bread.

God is like that. He's so different than us. When we're scared and weak and defenseless, He's strong and powerful and sure. We can be certain of His great love for us because He tells us so. He tells the world that we're His children, and He lavishes us with good gifts.

Often God blesses me through other people. He sends me ginger krinkles from my sister, a squishy hug from a little one, and much-needed words of encouragement—all a special delivery at the precise moment I need them.

Sometimes He personally delivers sunshine to warm my skin after a long Canadian winter or sends the scent of lilacs wafting through my kitchen window as songbirds fill the air with their praises.

Girlfriend, we can be thankful that God promises we will never be alone. We are His:

"See what great love the Father has lavished on us, that we should be called children of God! And that is what we are! The reason the world does not know us is that it did not know him" (1 John 3:1).

No matter what we are facing, when fear creeps in and anxiety sets us on edge, we can thank God that He is absolutely "other" than us. And in that contrast lies our peace.

Listen, Sister: Are you struggling today? Thank God that He promises to stay by your side.

Rescue Mission

ry blades of grass pricked my soles as I wandered across the sunny yard. Out of the corner of my eye, a fluttering on the ground caught my attention. At my feet, a giant moth laboured to move through the grass. His magnificent wings sat folded on his back, useless to lift his plump sausage body off the ground. Perhaps he had been blown there by the blustery wind, and I imagined a rude awakening upon emerging from his sleepy cocoon.

Settling onto the cool sod, I watched, fascinated, encouraging him with kind words as he fought to climb each blade and leaf as though it were a treacherous mountain frontier. Girlfriend, I have been alone a lot lately.

After several minutes of cheerleading on my knees, an inquisitive ant found my friend to be an interesting meal and started to pick on him. Somehow, this didn't seem right to me. The moth and I had been forging a bond for some time now, so I stepped up to protect God's creature as I kindly, gently coaxed him onto a stick, all the while explaining the rescue mission. Once we reached the patio, I positioned my little buddy in the warm sunshine where his exquisite wings could dry and prepare for his first flight.

I imagined him soaring in the skies in all his splendor and thanking me, from the depths of his tiny moth heart, for saving his life.

My heart swelled with pride for a deed well done as I turned and walked away. Suddenly, a loud flapping filled the air. In absolute horror, I turned just in time to see a hungry bird swoop in and snatch my plump, juicy moth for his easy lunch.

Have you ever been convinced that you should help, only to face shock and confusion when things don't turn out the way you planned?

Insects aside, it is difficult to watch the people we love struggle. By nature, I'm a problem solver. I often fly to rescue my people from their hard situations. It's just what I do.

But I'm reminded of the line graph of my personal mountains and valleys. It was during the lowest times, the most difficult trials, that I learned the most. Without pain, there is no growth. It was in the darkest hours, with nowhere else to turn, that my relationship with God was forged solid and I learned to cling to my only hope. He is our rescuer:

"Is anyone crying for help? God is listening, ready to rescue you. If your heart is broken, you'll find God right there; if you're kicked in the gut, he'll help you catch your breath" (Ps. 34:17–18, MSG).

Listen, Sister: Maybe we're not designed to be the rescuer. Let's be the encourager. Let's be the revealer. Let's point the strugglers to the true rescuer, Christ, the only one who offers hope.

Special Delivery

My relationship with my brother Jack has progressed through many stages, as is likely common in families where the firstborn sister is usually right and her little brother is learning how to live with that.

We were in one of those stages where the only hope for restoring our relationship was either maturity or living apart. Likely it was the latter. After I moved out, settling in the very next town, Jack, the brains of the family, attended university a couple of hours away.

Just when we finally gained a strong connection, he decided to pursue the love of his life clear across the country. As I watched him cram his earthly possessions, lock, stock, and barrel, into his trusty Zephyr, he bequeathed to me Spot, his beloved piranha. I imagine he considered my mothering skills and nurturing personality when assigning Spot to my care. Clearly, it was a mistake.

Spot was a loner. He spent his life swimming in circles around his dirty aquarium in the upper bedroom of the drafty, old farmhouse. Of course, it would have been a much cleaner tank if he hadn't gobbled up the algae eater. His seemed like a miserable existence, which is likely why he soon gave up his will to live and I found him floating belly up.

Enter Tess's plan:

- Jack is a million miles away and likely missing me.
- Jack loves to get mail, and a package would be entertaining and encouraging for him.
- Jack loves his fish.

This is how genius ideas are born.

As I carefully prepared Spot for his final voyage, I enveloped him in a layer of wax, placed him in a plastic container, and made sure to burp the lid. Obviously. Tupperware had never failed me, always providing a tight seal and a freshness guarantee.

A week later and across the country, Jack received the notice of a parcel. I'm sure his heart soared. I knew it would. I *am* a good sister. This was back in the day before emails and cell phones, and Canada Post was our only real lifeline.

I imagine him elated, rushing across campus to retrieve his box. Homemade cookies? Words of encouragement? Oh, he had no idea.

As he rounded the corner, an oppressive odour caught him off guard, the kind of foul stench that forces bile up your throat and into your mouth. *Whoa. What died out here?*

Rushing inside, the nasty smell intensified, an overbearing weight. Swallowing hard as he approached the counter, Jack shared the discomfort evident on the faces of clerks and customers alike.

Visibly relieved, the attendant handed over the stinky package. I wonder if she remembers the moment to this day.

Girlfriend, my intentions were honourable. I had in mind to send my brother a unique gift, a memory from home, something to make him laugh and let him know we were thinking of him.

This isn't the first or the last time my good intentions fell flat. Thankfully, Jack has a fantastic—if somewhat warped—sense of humour, and he did eventually forgive me.

I'm thankful for unending grace from God and also some from my brother, Jack. My plan may not have panned out exactly the way I envisioned, but we've laughed about it on several occasions. And laughter does the soul good as we're told in Proverbs:

> "A joyful heart is good medicine, but a crushed spirit dries up the bones" (17:22, ESV).

Listen, Sister: When you're struggling with the actions of a friend, when their comments or decisions rub you the wrong way, it's always advisable to consider their intentions. Grace is a prerequisite of every close relationship between imperfect human beings.

Radiant

I'm not a big fan of autumn. But I discovered something this week that I hope will stick in my mind every time the leaves fall.

Personally, I prefer summer. Soaking up rays poolside, sunset strolls on a sandy beach, and absolutely every food barbecued are my favourite things.

Fall, on the other hand, has only three redeeming qualities.

- Shipping the kids off to school.
- Enjoying magnificent autumn colours.
- Remembering every day is one day closer to next summer.

I've wondered if God gave Canadians the gift of beautiful trees as sort of a consolation prize: "Sorry summer is over and dreadful winter is on its way; perhaps this will numb the pain."

It turns out there is some interesting science behind the changing of the leaves. I recently learned that those exquisite fall colours have been hanging out in the leaves all along. (Who knew?) These brilliant hues are concealed within the leaf by green chlorophyll. As the weather cools and the days grow shorter, the tree breaks up the chlorophyll in the leaf, sending the nutrients to the root. As it breaks up, the green gives way to the brilliant yellows, vibrant oranges, and blazing reds hiding beneath.

Maybe this is an interesting picture of us.

Even though I'm a Jesus girl and His Spirit lives in me, I'm also masked on the outside by my own "greenness." Parts of me are fighting tooth and nail with old habits, like surging pride and weak-kneed faith.

God is changing me bit by bit. Praise the Lord! I want my true colours to be visible. I want to be radiant, don't you?

This doesn't happen overnight. And it's terribly painful. Our old nature is stuck like sticky pine sap. And at times it appears I'm a solid green leaf with no autumn colour in sight.

But what God says is true. We (His girls) reflect God's glory as He is transforming us into His likeness. Can you even imagine? Second Corinthians proclaims this astounding promise:

> "And when God is personally present, a living Spirit, that old, constricting legislation is recognized as obsolete. We're free of it! All of us! Nothing between us and God, our faces shining with the brightness of his face. And so we are transfigured much like the Messiah, our lives gradually becoming brighter and more beautiful as God enters our lives and we become like him" (3:17–18, MSG).

Listen, Sister: Let's pray that God will reveal His new life in us, that He will grow us and change us and make us more and more like Him. Let's trust the old pieces will shrivel up and die to make way, bit by bit and day by day, for the glorious, radiant Spirit to shine through us.

Spitting Image

Do you remember this wild and wacky Ray Stevens classic, "Guitarzan"?

He's free as the breeze;

He's always at ease.

He lives in the jungle and hangs by his knees,

As he swings through trees

Without a trapeze in his BVDs.

"Guitarzan" is a silly song about Tarzan, his wife, and a gorilla who likes to have a little nip and sing his heart out. But for me, this song conjures up an even funnier memory.

It was my parents' twenty-fifth anniversary party. During the "skit" part of the celebration (we have a fun family), three of us re-enacted this very song. It was not much of a professional production, and an open bar was likely the only thing saving us from rotten tomatoes.

The highlight of the show was my brother in a dress. This, notably, is not as uncommon as you may think. He was a tall, lanky drink of water, and the dress barely covered his rump.

As planned during our grand performance, "Jane" took a swig from the little brown jug. My brother, parched from singing his heart out, eagerly sucked back a substantial amount of liquid. But instead of a cool refreshing drink, he was shocked to discover some sort of bootleg firewater scorching its way down his throat.

As quickly as he guzzled it down, he spewed it right back out, showering the first row of spectators.

This hilarious scene (perhaps less entertaining to him) came to mind this week, over thirty years later, as I grabbed a coffee and took a swig.

Now, I love piping hot coffee. I also love iced coffee. But I think you will agree that anywhere in between just isn't satisfying at all.

In Revelation, God described the church people as "lukewarm." They were getting along just fine in life and forgot they needed God at all. But instead of rich and successful, He told them they were wretched, pitiful, poor, blind, and naked. He was about to spew them out of His mouth. Yikes!

The thought of God wanting to spit me out of His mouth is terrifying.

So, let's take a little look at ourselves. Are you self-reliant? Have you forgotten how desperately you need God? Have you lost touch with Him in the busyness of life? Or would you describe yourself as "on fire" for Jesus?

I'm not talking about your collection of "I heart Jesus" T-shirts or "Fueled by the Spirit" coffee mugs. I'm thinking about what people see in us. As Christ-followers, we're different than the rest of the world. We are children of the Light.

So, here's the question: would the people who run into you—your coworkers, cashiers, the drivers who cut you off—see you as different than the next Tom, Dick, or Harry?

We want everyone to see evidence of the Spirit living in us. We want God to be glorified by the things we do and say.

Let me tell you, I am far from good at this. Lord, help me.

Our responses, our compassion, how we cope, and how we love all point to Jesus. This isn't a show or a set of rules we need to follow. This is the automatic outpouring of Jesus in our lives, the running over of God's love. It can't be held back but bubbles onto everyone around us.

And if we don't see evidence of this, then maybe we need to plug in, recharge, and spend more time with the source of our hope. The closer we are with our heavenly Father, reading His Word and listening to Him, the more we will look like Him:

> "But the fruit of the Spirit is love, joy, peace, patience, kindness, goodness, faithfulness, gentleness, self-control; against such things there is no law" (Gal. 5:22-23, NASB).

I'll take bubbling over spewing any day.

Listen, Sister: Are you plugged in to Jesus? Open the Bible every day and spend time basking in hope.

Love Them All

I'm kind of a nature nut; I love all of God's creation. Or so I would have said until a wee visitor showed up today and changed my mind.

You see, I love to watch robins tilt their heads slightly in the moments before they pluck the unsuspecting worm from the grassy lawn. I revel in the vast shades of green in plants, bushes, and trees in my panoramic backyard view, and I marvel at the morning glories sneaking up imperceptibly, latching on to the next rung of the trellis.

Today as I sat at my patio table, basking in welcome sunshine, a mouse scurried out from behind the rain barrel across the yard. I jumped. Our eyes locked, his black and beady and mine wide in terror.

Instantly I lifted my feet up off the ground to discourage any attempt the small rodent may make to run across the lawn, onto the patio, and up my leg. You can't be too careful. Mice terrify me.

He had a long, thick, hairy tail and a roly-poly tummy. The more I think about it, he may have actually been a rat. But when I squealed, "It's a mouse; it's a mouse; it's a mouse," in my high-pitched, panic-stricken voice, he did not correct me.

So, I guess I love to see some but not *all* of nature.

Are we selective like this in other, more important, areas of our lives? For instance, when God asks us to love everyone, am I selective in who I decide to apply that to?

It's easy to love our friends, our family, and, most times, even our teenagers, but we are called to love everyone. That's a stretch, isn't it?

Do we love the guy down the street who is hungry because he spends every cent on drugs to numb his pain? Do we love the girl whose terrible choices led to the end of her marriage? How about the unwed teen, belly round with new life, or the heartbroken woman in shame and regret after ending her baby's life?

We don't get to choose. It's brutally hard. Sure, it sounds good on paper. I can say it, text it, tweet it, make a pretty post on Insta: "Love 'em all, yada, yada." But when we come face to face with a living person, when they stare back at us with hollow eyes, void of hope, this is where the rubber meets the road.

What does love look like? Is it feeding the hungry, hugging the lonely, or listening to the story of every hurting person? It can be any of those things and more, but we are absolutely called to a life of love:

"A new command I give you: Love one another. As I have loved you, so you must love one another" (John 13:14).

I want to do this. I really do. Don't you? I want to love everyone. And yet, I struggle. I have an organized, regimented personality. I thrive on systems; I love to have a schedule and hold to it. So, I'm trying to learn to be more flexible, to ask God for opportunities and the eyes to see them. I'm asking Him to give me the margin to love on people when the moments arise. If you do this, my friend, God will blow your mind. You will see doors open and situations appear, giving you unexpected chances to love people.

Alone, we can't change the world. But with God's help, we can change lives, love on people, and point them to the only hope, the hope of Jesus.

Listen, Sister: Ask God today to show you an opportunity to share hope with one person.

Looking Back

B ack in the early years of our freakshow family, we had a lot of bodies and not a lot of money. We couldn't afford the classic home-school van, which is likely for the best. Watching perfectly behaved youngsters pour out of those vehicles for years may well have set the bar too high for our blending family. Instead, we ended up with a real prize worth squabbling for.

To transport our entire family to any group event, we simply took two vehicles. Church, sports, and family functions all had the kids clamouring for their turn in my favourite, the blessed station wagon.

Although this little honey of a car didn't feature the simulated wood grain design—but would have been retro-cool if it had—it did seat seven in relative comfort. The feature that had the kids fighting for their turn was the rear-faced seating in the hatch. This was super cool for both children and parents.

Buckled in safely, they stared, two at a time, out the back window, watching where they had been. Girlfriend, if you were a driver of one of those vehicles following me down the road back then, let me stop right here and apologize for the onslaught of funny faces, tongue protrusions, hand signals, and incessant waving coming from the back hatch of my car.

From my viewpoint, the jump seat was a valuable feature, well worth the initial conflict it created. Sitting in the driver's seat, I could hear nothing that emanated from back there. Any type of noise that did ramp up or got annoying could easily be drown out by simply turning up the volume on the cassette player with yet another run-through of *Silly Songs with Larry*.

For obvious reasons, the station wagon hatch opened only from the outside, which likely saved their little lives. This feature allowed me an entire fifteen seconds of peace as I disembarked the car and before letting the little darlings out. Heaven.

I was having a conversation the other day with my oldest. He never got to experience the rear-facing jump seat, having aged out of the freakshow well ahead of the station-wagon era. My talk with him did center around the past, though. My soul was aching with regret and mistakes, triggered by the enemy as he tried to load my mind with sadness and guilt. I beat myself up for my less-than-stellar mothering decisions and stand in amazement at the great dad he is. As I poured out my heart in deep-seated remorse, pain dripping through my words—and also from my eyes—he told me something I will never forget: "Mom, you can't move forward if you're continually looking back."

Bam!

I had already worked through this anguish and regret years ago, with great pain. I had taken ownership of my mistakes, the hurt I caused him, and asked for forgiveness. His forgiveness was healing for both of us. He's an outstanding son. Yet, I returned, time and time again, to feelings of disgrace and insecurity. I was swept backwards, rear-facing.

Does this sound familiar to you? Is your heart sick, continuing to dwell on a past that is already forgiven? Is the enemy distracting your attention from your calling today by pointing out your screw-ups from yesterday? Yet, Jesus promises us we are free once and for all, with no reason to doubt:

"So if the Son sets you free, you will be free indeed" (John 8:36).

Listen, Sister: Let's be free. Once we confess our sin to God, He forgives it and banishes it away forever. He never thinks of it again. Why would you want to keep bringing it up, volunteering to be trapped in that seat, buckled in and facing the wrong direction?

Energy Denied

I'm thankful we could raise our kids in a little village where people knew one another by name and where secrets were nearly impossible.

Our son TJ was in grade four of the special needs class in the public school just down the street. His ragtag band of friends was doing life together through the years in that little schoolroom under the wings of the most extraordinarily patient teacher. Girlfriend, all teachers deserve a medal, but teachers of these exceptional kids deserve a significant reward in heaven. It's not a vocation for the weak of heart.

Our family had recently learned of TJ's suspected FASD diagnosis, and although devastating, it did help us understand his erratic behaviours and poor choices; it also prepared us to adjust our expectations. He was lively and full of stories and gave that dear teacher a run for her money.

Our town boasted one sole variety store on the main drag, a hot spot for hand-dipped ice cream cones and rented movies. One afternoon, I got a call from the clerk.

"Is this TJ's mom?"

What has the boy done now? Calls like this were neither rare nor enjoyable.

The clerk proceeded to explain our son had just left the store after trying to buy a giant energy drink with a crispy, new twenty-dollar bill, and she was suspicious.

Justifying her refusal to sell him the can of liquid caffeine, she explained, "I didn't think you let him have energy drinks."

"Or twenty-dollar bills!" I agreed.

After moseying around town for a bit, the boy eventually appeared in the backyard with a pop and a couple of slices of pizza: one for him and one for his little brother. I guess he was determined to spend his fortune.

Relaying the details of the day, he reported on a class trip to the bank where the students learned how to withdraw cash from their accounts. It was all making sense now. He was simply trying out his new skill. And he was generous at the same time. Let's call this a win.

I'm still thankful for the call; the clerk was bang-on to make me aware. And this little guy's body hopped up on fluid energy would, without question, be asking for trouble.

Raising TJ in our tight-knit community, where everyone knew him by name, was a great experience. Teachers, neighbours, and friends who looked out for him and cared about him, forgiving frequent offenses, made all the difference. We all need a group of people to encourage us and put us in check when we need it:

"Brothers and sisters, we urge you to warn those who are lazy. Encourage those who are timid. Take tender care of those who are weak. Be patient with everyone" (1 Thess. 5:14, NLT).

Listen, Sister: Are you feeding into the next generation, generously giving what you can, mentoring and teaching? Whether it's your block, your church community, or your friends who feel like family, support them, watch out for them, and raise up a strong generation who loves God.

Living Unaware

I grew up reading mystery novels and pride myself on keeping a keen eye as I go about my day. Situational awareness, my husband calls it. As a matter of fact, I mentioned to my youngest just this week that I think I resemble Nancy Drew, the brilliant teenage sleuth. He's convinced I'm more like Inspector Gadget, the haphazard, fumbling cartoon detective. He's not wrong.

Recently, I was thinking about the wedding Jesus attended in Cana long ago and how his mom, Mary, noticed the wine supply was getting low. Mary was not only in attendance, but she was in tune with the activities happening all around her. She gave her full attention to other people and developing situations during the festivities.

Imagine if this scene took place in present-day North America. After months of planning, choosing the perfect venue, and saying yes to the dress, the wedding day finally arrives. Soft hues, delicate lighting, and exquisite bouquets fill the room as joyful guests mingle, sharing a glass of wine. In the corner, beside the head table, sits a collection of memories, funny pictures and mementos from the couple's journey together so far. Standing beside this table is a young girl.

At first glance, it appears our girl is glancing at the display, enjoying the story of young love. But don't be fooled. She is, in fact, looking down, absorbed in her cellphone. For the remainder of the celebration, instead of being aware and involved in the world unfolding before her, she's taking pictures of the food, uploading duck-lip selfies, and sharing videos on social media. She has no idea of the needs, or sometimes the existence, of the other guests around her.

Have you ever been there, Sister? I sure have. I've been frustrated at a certain (unnamed) man who lives here with me as he's unable to listen because his brain is tuned into his cell. And truthfully, too often I find myself also sucked into this hand-held realm and oblivious to the real world around me

Are we so self-focused, so oblivious to the world around us, that we miss the most important things? Lord, have mercy.

Girlfriend, God wants us to be a light to the world, to love on lonely people, and to spread hope to the hopeless. How can we do that if we don't bother trying to see them? What a shallow, pointless existence if we are self-focused and unable to engage with anyone else.

Don't you want to live a bigger life—bigger than you've ever lived, bigger than that device in your hand? Then take to heart Philippians 2:3–4:

"Do nothing from selfishness or empty conceit, but with humility consider one another as more important than yourselves; do not merely look out for your own personal interests, but also for the interests of others" (NASB).

Join me in this. God will bless your socks off.

Listen, Sister: Ask God to show you amazing things, to bring people into your life who are looking for hope, and to work in a mighty way through your obedience. I guarantee He will.

Little Dumpsters

R aising children is not for the cocky, and I've often wondered if God sent mine simply to cement humility permanently into my character.

I absolutely loved my babies, but at the same time, I was not disappointed to finally see the end of the infant-raising era. Babies are wonderful and a miracle and exhausting, and by the end of it, I was more than ready for a full night of sleep.

But the next stage is no picnic either, Sister. Teaching manners and sharing and potty training is overwhelming. Kids and their tantrums drain the energy right out of you,

We raised our family in a friendly little hamlet. It was country atmosphere with the luxury of sidewalks. We had it all. Our home was strategically located across from the ballpark and two doors down from the only grocery store.

Foodland was the hub of our small town. The smell of home-baked goodness filled the air as friends and neighbours chatted in the pristine aisles, sharing small-town gossip.

Charlie, the store owner, employed all the local teenagers and taught them to be friendly and kind. To this day, they bag food and lug it to the cars while engaging customers in friendly conversation. On more than one occasion, the staff carried mine all the way home since I lived close and was often overly optimistic when estimating how much my two hands could hold. These people are so kind.

One day as I stood in the store waiting my turn, I overheard two women talking about an interesting event they had witnessed in the grocery store parking lot. Apparently, two little boys were spotted, oblivious to the gathering crowd of spectators, squatting beside the dumpster pooping.

Initially, I smiled and snickered along. Oh, to be young and free. And then, steadily, a warm familiar wave of realization washed over me. A pre-menopausal hot flash encompassed my entire body, and the urge to bolt was irresistible. My face flushed crimson as I ran out the back door and across the yards to our house.

Interrogation masked as casual conversation revealed that it was indeed my two little boys' white bottoms turning heads and drawing smiles in the parking lot down the street.

The boys did not deny it. They coincidentally both needed to "go" at precisely the same moment. What are the odds? In their defense, I guess I hadn't laid out any non-pooping guidelines. As a mom, you just can't think of everything.

The apostle Paul tells us that we should be clothed in humility.

"Therefore, as God's chosen people, holy and dearly loved, clothe yourselves with compassion, kindness, humility, gentleness and patience" (Col. 3:12).

Listen, Sister: Our children are the joy of our lives, and every one of them is a gift. Thank God for working through them to keep you humble.

Listen to This

I didn't want to be there, helping a friend, volunteering when my own life was in shambles. I was holding on by a thread, hot tears just biding their time, teetering at the edge. One nudge, one unintentional bump threatened to burst open the floodgate. *Breathe*, I told myself, *just breathe*.

I kept my promise to help at the performance—not like I had anywhere else to go on a Saturday night. To be honest, I didn't have the strength to bail at the last minute and disappoint one more person.

As I prepared for the crowd, a man stumbled in from the street, glad for the shelter from the bitter cold. His pants were grubby and torn, and his old wool coat missed buttons that surely would have helped ward off the driving snow. Strings of grey hair peeked out from under his toque, and his tired eyes avoided my gaze as he plunked himself down at an empty table.

Just then the concert let out, flooding the lobby with lively show-goers stretching their legs during intermission. The air was thick with excitement as folks recognized friends in the small-town atmosphere. There were handshakes and hugs all around, a thick sense of community noticeable among the people who lingered waiting for the show to resume.

The man was invisible to every one of them, though his filthy, unshaven appearance screamed in contrast to their festive party attire. I watched in silence as the minutes ticked away; not one person seemed to notice him sitting there all alone.

One by one the joyful crowd emptied back into the theatre and the lobby returned to silence, an empty room with only me and him.

As I glanced over, compassion flooded my heart, stinging with every breath. Was he sad? Was he lonely? Was he angry? God nudged me, rattling my heart, pressing me to talk to this stranger.

Lord, how can I love this man? Does he need money, food, or a warm place to stay? Oh, boy. Please show me.

As I approached his table, the man spoke. I dragged a chair over and slid into it, peering deep into his eyes. I heard a lot from my new friend that night; he talked for a long while in a gravelly voice. And I listened. He shared stories of his life, crazy, shocking, rough experiences and sad, unfair, gut-wrenching tales. He spoke not in a complaining way but like there were a million words pent up inside his soul, longing to be freed. I didn't say one word.

Abruptly, he stood up, pulled his hat down over his ears, and walked out. I guess he got what he needed.

Girlfriend, have you ever longed to be heard? Have you enjoyed the encouragement of a listening ear?

If I'm honest, I'm usually less of a listener and more of a talker. My gut response is to solve problems and give advice. Sometimes part of my brain is researching a successful solution while the other half is working to tune in to the hurting person. I'm learning that this is not always the best strategy, and Proverbs confirms:

"To answer before listening—that is folly and shame" (18:13).

Listen, Sister: Let's determine today to listen to the stories of others. Let's provide a shoulder to cry on and a compassionate, attentive heart.

Let's Just See If It Sticks

My pure, white gown cascades spotless and brilliant against the memory of my pitch-black past.

Not everyone is as excited about my redemption as I am. Although I had chosen to follow Christ early in life, I later walked the other way—far the other way. I made terrible decisions and basically ruined life for a lot of people. By the time the dust cleared, the wreckage was too painful to look at. Although I knew the truth and realized I had no hope without God, I felt like I was too far gone. There was no coming back. So, I lived agonizing years trapped in shame and regret. And the outward carnage couldn't hold a candle to the war at work inside my brain.

My road back to following God was neither smooth nor easy. My choices had brought significant pain to many people, and taking ownership of that was excruciating.

But step by baby step, by God's grace, I grew. In obedience, I asked for forgiveness from those I had hurt terribly. Miraculously, God healed relationships and blew my mind, time after time. The Lord is full of mercy, choosing not to give us what we justly deserve and instead giving each of us grace, piling favour on us that we can never repay.

Living in a small community at the time, I often ran into women from my old church. I could recognize them a mile away. Although they had shed the square lace collars, their demeanors dripped thick with judgment, and accusations shot like shards of glass with each accusatory glance. Also, they literally crossed the street to avoid me.

Many times, I attempted to engage these former friends but was rejected instead as one with leprous skin. I even invented a game of speaking to these ladies in public, forcing them to answer politely to save face in front of cashiers and librarians. Perhaps it was sort of a "heap burning coals" type of strategy. At the time, I called it survival.

Girlfriend, my challenge is this: how are we responding to women returning to Jesus? I'm referring to the girls caught in sin, having made terrible decisions and now drowning in regret, the ones trampled by the enemy each time they try to lift their head from the asphalt. Are we staring, watching for a chance to kick them in the teeth or laying odds on their ability to successfully escape their life of sin? As far as I can understand, our mission is not to stand in judgment, weighing out the level of godliness of any person. Our mission is only to love. Believe me when I say, none of us need more condemnation piled on our hearts.

To be honest, the enemy used those deprecating women years ago to heap bucket loads of shame on my paper thin, already forgiven heart to discourage me, and at times, I lost hope.

But God. God sent new friends, godly women to mentor me, love me, and accept me as I was, absolutely free and forgiven. They praised God with me for His rescue mission to this one lost lamb returning to the fold. They lived like they believed Ephesians 2:8–9, that we are all just sinners saved by grace:

"For it is by grace you have been saved, through faith—and this is not from yourselves, it is the gift of God—not by works, so that no one can boast." I'm forever grateful.

Listen, Sister: Let's join the cheering squad. We don't need to know her details, and I cannot find any verse in my Bible that says, "Let's see if it sticks first." Praise God, for He has rescued one wayward soul back into the fold. Thank God for His mercy on each one of us. Without it, who could stand? Let's be that kind of friend.

Known

He sauntered into the pub, exhausted after a long day, and instantly the room roared in unison: "Norm!"

This iconic scene from the old TV series *Cheers* reminds me we all truly long to be known. Can't we all identify with this? How sweet it sounds for our tribe, our peeps, to call us by name.

Back in the day—and I prefer it, let me tell you—we met most often in real life. Face-to-face gab sessions took place around the kitchen table. We were doing life together, sharing struggles and victories over a bowl of Doritos. I loved hanging with my gang of girls, and I loved being known.

This burning hunger to be known is an innate desire woven deep within us by our Creator. It's a marvelous feeling to be recognized, to be welcomed in by those who love us.

Today, we often see this manifest in social media. We're posting and checking, re-checking with bated breath, longing for likes, and counting an abacus of followers and friends.

Listen, Sister, we are already known. We don't need to struggle for attention, to fight for followers and fake friends. We're fully known by our Creator. He is the answer to our deepest longing. He knows us intimately and loves us still. *This* blows my mind.

It's true. God sees within us. He knows every secret thought in your head, every reaction in the dark, every hope you barely latch on to, and the dream you dare not speak out loud.

Pastor of Redeemer Presbyterian Church in New York City, Timothy Keller writes of how God knows His children: "To be loved but not known is comforting but superficial. To be known and not loved is our greatest fear. But to be fully known and truly loved is, well, a lot like being loved by God. It is what we need more than anything. It liberates us from pretense, humbles us out of our self-righteousness, and fortifies us for any difficulty life can throw at us" (*The Meaning of Marriage: Facing the Complexities of Commitment with the Wisdom of God*, Penguin, 2011). And Paul confirms this supernatural relationship in his letter to the Corinthians:

"But if anyone loves God, he is known by God" (1 Cor. 8:3).

And not only does God love us, but He also delights in us. Tenderly, He sings over us, like a mama lullabies whispered songs of peace over her newborn babe. Oh, how I need to remember this.

He longs to meet with us, to hang out and listen, to speak acceptance and understanding.

Listen, Sister: Let's take a load off. With God, there is no pretense. He's waiting to hear from you. Whether you chat with Him often or it's been a very long time—or maybe you've never spoken to Him before—you can come as you are. Wear your track pants, no filters, no faking. You are welcome in.

Just Pedal

I possess many traits of a successful entrepreneur. I have a strong work ethic, people skills, passion, determination, and discipline. Now that I think of it, I've consistently had some kind of side gig going most of my life. I believe it's this sense of adventure that makes me a fun, well-rounded person. And it's most likely my aversion to details and lack of planning that keep me inconspicuous and humble. Not all my ideas are winners.

For example, I've always dreamed of having an ice cream bike. Not a bike made of ice cream—that would be ridiculous (and yummy)—but a travelling ice cream store mounted on a bicycle delivering frozen goodness to the delighted masses.

Growing up in the middle of nowhere, this sort of thing existed only in our imaginations, fueled by Saturday morning cartoons and books from the library. It sounded magical.

So, when I came upon a used one for sale online, I was all in. At the time, I was in between marriages and had no level-headed partner to talk me out of these sorts of ideas. Yes, let's blame that.

I had to travel a few hours to pick it up, and somehow, I talked a friend into volunteering his truck. God bless men with pickup trucks. Looking back, there were some clear warning signs right away. The equipment was sketchy at best and not as described. But my plan would not be thwarted. Also, my plan did not include details and necessary logistical components, such as a driver and a method to keep the ice cream cold. As it turned out, there was no freezer unit. Surprised? Yes, me too.

As the summer progressed, we worked through some kinks and hired a second driver, a young girl who was as sweet as the ice cream itself. The kids had the freedom to travel any route they chose, and we all prayed for sunshine.

On the day of her maiden cruise, my phone rang at work. On the other end, I could barely make out the quivering voice of my newest ice cream clerk.

"I can't do this . . . I'm scared!"

My mind raced with terrifying scenarios. Maybe she was apprehended by a gang of thugs who beat her up for money and popsicles. Or perhaps irate parents rallied against her, shouting insults, all up in arms about the sugar intake of their kiddos. Or maybe she had used every bit of energy to pedal the cumbersome bike to the top of the overpass and looked down, terror-stricken, afraid to crash or steer into traffic.

"Where are you?" I held my breath and listened closely.

"I'm in your driveway."

She hadn't started. She was frozen in place by the fear to move forward. She just needed to pedal, but she was powerless to do it.

Can you relate? Has anxiety ever seized your heart, making it impossible to move forward and even difficult to breathe?

Girlfriend, God knew this would happen. That's why He tells us 365 times in the Bible to fear not—once for every single day of the year. That message was for army commanders, pregnant teenagers, mourning widows, and Jesus followers.

When God asks us to do something, He knows we will be afraid, so He promises to never leave our side. Personally, my process (and I don't recommend it) looks something like this:

- I think God is asking me to do the thing.
- I doubt it, so I ask God to tell me clearly so I don't do the wrong thing, inviting catastrophe.
- Time passes, and I'm sure now that God is asking me to do the thing.
- I doubt I can do it, so I argue, beg, and make suggestions to God of other people who are better at the thing than me.
- Finally, I start by doing only the very next step.

That last step is where I am at least some of the time now: learning to do the next thing today. I'm not trying for the perfect thing or the whole thing but the next thing. I am constantly remembering the promise of 2 Timothy 3:16–17, that He has equipped me for all He's called me to do:

"All Scripture is God-breathed and is useful for teaching, rebuking, correcting and training in righteousness, so that the servant of God may be thoroughly equipped for every good work."

Listen, Sister: God has got your back, and He promises that He will equip you for the things that He has called you to do, one day, one hour at a time. You just need to pedal.

Every Stone Has a Name

Here lies Henry Blake. He stepped on the gas instead of the brake.

After my dad died a few years ago, we placed a granite stone on his grave to commemorate his life. We wanted a permanent headstone to mark his place, although I don't believe he is actually hanging out there. More important, we yearned for a lasting record of his short time in history: Doug Hollingsworth, 1942–2018.

As a family, we discussed the various engraving styles and options available. It was a "monumental decision," you might say. We all agreed the stone needed to accurately reflect the life he lived, and that was not an easy task.

We threw around plenty of image ideas, like a transport truck since he steered eighteen wheelers so many miles; roses for his love of gardening; and even a town crest in honour of his work in local politics and service clubs. Finally, we settled on a little Massey Ferguson tractor since he was a farmer at heart and puttering along in the field encompassed both his love for the land and his most common rate of speed most of his life.

Wandering around in the tranquil shade of the graveyard, I read stone after stone. I saw lives snuffed short or surviving a century long; I noticed teen soldiers who lost their lives, babies only days old, and widows who waited decades to take their place.

Every precious person, every name carved in stone was once, like us, a living, breathing human. They lived, loved, and likely paid little mind to the words that would one day complete their epitaph. The truth is, we each have but one life, with no do-overs. Not one of us has more than twenty-four hours a day to live, to make a difference, or to change the world.

Girlfriend, someday our own memorial stone will testify to our lives: birth–death. But it's the dash between that counts, isn't it? It's the life we've lived, the love we've poured out, and the mercy we've offered that really matter. That's why Paul cautioned the Ephesians to

"Be very careful, then, how you live—not as unwise but as wise, making the most of every opportunity, because the days are evil" (Eph. 5:15–16).

I imagine the scene after my own funeral when family and friends are gathered around, eating quarter-cut egg salad sandwiches and drinking weak coffee from Styrofoam cups. Maybe they will laugh and reminisce about the embarrassing things I did or the awkward experiences we shared. I hope they mention they felt loved and treasured by me.

I bet not one person will remark on my slender waist, blemish-free complexion, or my ability to avoid surprise flatulence. So why do I pay any mind to these things while I'm still alive? What a waste of precious time.

Listen, Sister: Let's live big. Let's make a difference in this world. Let's not sit around and wait for tomorrow. Let's give those girls coming after us oodles to talk about. Because in the end, it's the dash that counts. Let's make it a thick, wavy line.

If Only There Was a Gauge

Life with kids can be lively and hectic and frequently out of control. Consistently all the littles need attention at precisely the same time, and the perpetual whining can grate on a mama's last nerve. Add to that the essential art of multi-tasking and a post-partum brain, and we've set the stage for the first time I lost my Mother of the Year nomination.

It was the dead of winter, and snow blew steadily across the highway as I headed home, my kids in tow. The baby, a few weeks old, was stuffed in a puffy polyester snowsuit and carefully buckled in the center row. Next, sat our little toe-head, not yet two, and our oldest son, a whopping six years old and all grown up. Often, I leaned on him as my helper, and in reflection, I realize just how young he was. Such is the plight of the first-born, I guess.

Our days were divided into four-hour segments in keeping with nursing times, and the baby was making it known, in no uncertain terms, that we were running behind schedule.

Whether the brothers were singing or fighting, I don't remember, but the youngest was undeniably wailing bloody murder from the back seat. Around that time, I recognized the soggy, warm sensation of milk making itself available through the front of my shirt below the winter layers. Lovely.

I leaned harder into the gas pedal, but instead of speeding up, the van slowed, ever so painfully, to a full stop on the edge of the road. This was not good news. Yet there I was, soaking wet and out of gas in January on a highway with three kids.

We poured out of the van into the bitter cold and trudged across the ditch through the drifts to the nearest house in search of a phone. I won't tell you how we got our wee babe over the wire fence, but despite all that, he survived. I can report he's alive and well today.

How could I run out of gas? There was a gauge right there in front of my face, right? Yes, this was needlessly pointed out to me after the fact. The truth is, I was distracted. Can you relate?

Have you ever been busy, on task with something important, and an unexpected interruption jumps in, demanding your immediate attention? Sometimes those distractions are legitimate demands on our attention: hungry babies, alarm clocks, or full bladders with a sneeze coming on. But lately, I am most often distracted by a piece of technology small enough to fit in my pocket. I can be mid-sentence, and at the sound of a beep, I lose concentration and battle the desire to automatically look at my phone, giving it the power to trump all other activity and supersede even face-to-face communication.

God has us here for a purpose. He wants us to be in relationship with Him. He has important things to teach us and wants to give us meaningful directions:

"My sheep listen to my voice; I know them, and they follow me. I give them eternal life, and they shall never perish; no one will snatch them out of my hand" (John 10:27–28).

Listen, Sister: Let's not miss His voice. He wants to communicate with us every day. I certainly don't want to miss that opportunity just because I'm distracted. Do you?

Comment Below

Have you ever read a social media post and felt the overwhelming desire to chime in? Perhaps it's an opinion different from your own or information that is blatantly inaccurate. An inner voice often urges me to resist, but it competes with a strong need to enlighten the author.

First off, let me say that I am not a fan of social media. As I've mentioned more than once, I much prefer real-life, face-to-face conversations. I delight in one-on-one chats with my BFF, discussing important world issues or (almost certainly) PMS-driven marital frustrations. I'm crazy about my rowdy Rummoli girls with their bulging bags of nickels and nacho dip in tow. But alas, social media is here to stay, and Facebook is a buzz of communication for better or for worse.

One of the complications that I've noticed with discussions on social platforms is our lack of accountability. Folks feel free to express any opinion and make brash statements they would never dare speak to a friend's sweet face. Have you, like me, cringed at those mean girl comments? I myself have written a well-intentioned reply that appeared downright friendly in my head, only to reread it later to my own horror.

Continually, I tell myself, *Tess, do not get sucked in*. But inevitably, I discover a post that I'm certain is simply not true. Horns and whistles scream relentlessly in my mind. As a "firstborn," I am convinced it is my God-given responsibility to set this person straight. (*Note: At this time, I have not yet been able to find the biblical reference to support this.)

On most occasions, the issue at hand is not a deep theological debate or anything of eternal value. The heated discussions have surrounded government rules, the actual income of landed immigrants as compared to our veterans, and also which canine is your spirit dog. But social media conversations are designed to elicit emotion; they're on mission to divide us, aren't they?

It seems quite an army of Facebook soldiers vocalize opinions and pass judgment on friends and neighbours, real and virtual. Whoever said words would never hurt us didn't log in on a regular basis. We don't all agree, and we never will. This fact is not newsworthy.

I'm not suggesting that commenting on a post is wrong. Heaven knows encouraging comments can be like a cool drink of water to a parched throat.

So, Girlfriend, when you and I feel compelled to add our two cents, here are some guidelines:

- Pause. An emotional response right out of the gate is often regrettable.
- Choose kind words.
- Show grace.
- Speak the truth in love.

Let that last point sink in. We are to show love to everyone—even our Facebook "friends":

"By this everyone will know that you are my disciples, if you love one another" (John 13:35).

Listen, Sister: Supporting each other is crucial. Facebook must agree as they rolled out an emoji for just such a thing. And when you choose this smiley yellow guy hugging a heart, comments are always optional.

I Know You

Once you've been married a while, even if your marriage has suffered some sputters and stalls over that time, you've likely grown to know your partner pretty well.

No doubt you've learned, like me, that men and women are entirely different. Well, my friend, this is the very truth that got me into a heap of trouble.

In my humble opinion, there must be a correlation between high testosterone and poor eyesight. So, when Ricky was having an issue finding a sleeping bag, I jumped in with both feet to help. He, however, was not at all interested in my assistance. Perhaps stubbornness can also be listed as a predominately male trait.

In our house, we have a dark, creepy room in the basement called the cold storage room. This crowded closet has no windows or lights, and piles of stuff we seldom use have been stuffed into the cramped, dank space. I felt certain the sleeping bag was in there.

Declining my help and searching by himself, my husband soon returned upstairs, reporting no success in finding the missing item. But I knew it was there. I wanted to push him aside and rush down to get it, partly to prove I was right but also to prove he was wrong. But, Sister, I'm practicing being a Proverbs 31 wife. So, no.

I waited a moment and nonchalantly headed for the stairs as my husband looked me in the eyes and slowly and deliberately said, "Do. Not."

He was grumpy from searching in vain, and I guess proving myself right was a blow he just couldn't take. So, I sat back down and agreed to abandon the search. For now.

Eventually, and according to schedule, Ricky prepared to go downstairs and take a shower. He stopped first at my chair and reminded me *not* to check the cold storage room because he had already done so, and then he went on about how he knows me so well or something like that. I stopped listening.

I did not go down. For three whole minutes.

Listening for the bathroom door to close, I allowed sufficient time for my husband to undress. I didn't need to allow time for glances in the bathroom mirror because, well, he's a guy—a definite advantage. Soon I heard the water running; he was in the shower.

On tippy-toes, I slowly and cautiously crept down the stairs. My heart hammered in my chest. Holding my breath, I inched past the bathroom door; the water continued.

I backed my way through the laundry room, never taking my eyes off the closed bathroom door. My senses were heightened, terrified I would get caught.

Finally, I reached the storage room. Steadily, I turned and pried the closet door open. And there, standing bigger than life was my husband.

"*Hey!*" he shouted as he lurched toward me.

I jumped clear out of my skin, heard myself scream, and peed my pants just a little.

But out of the corner of my eye, I spotted the sleeping bag on the top shelf.

Girlfriend, marriage isn't all fun and games but laughter is the crazy glue that holds our relationship together. We're told that

"A cheerful heart is good medicine, but a crushed spirit dries up the bones" (Prov. 17:22).

Listen, Sister: Intentionally add some fun and laughter to a relationship today.

Grandad

I didn't see it coming. The world was moving along, tickety-boo, and day in, day out, we were doing life. Our family isn't perfect, but our issues were regular, almost insignificant, in comparison to many. And then, out of the blue, *bam.* The bottom fell out of our world.

COVID-19 reared its ugly head and nearly everything in our lives changed overnight. We were sent home from work and school to watch the death toll climb on relentless news reports as playgrounds were roped off with bright-yellow caution tape.

Normally, I like to know what my day will look like ahead of time. I usually decide the menu for dinner before seven o'clock in the morning, and I complete household chores in a sensible order and on schedule like most sane people do, I suppose. But my world looks anything but normal right now. I struggle to put one foot in front of the other; I can't finish a complete thought; sleep is a long-lost memory.

A friend reached out to me, bitter and confused in her own world of churning chaos. "Where is God in all of this?" she asked. It didn't feel to her like God was near. Maybe He stepped away from the group chat and then all hell broke loose in her little corner of planet Earth.

But, no, of course, we know that isn't true. And God is never taken by surprise. He's aware of our situations, past, present, and future. Sometimes God does feel far away, but we know feelings are not truth, my friend. Let's search together for truth.

Deuteronomy 31:6 says, "Be strong. Take courage. Don't be intimidated. Don't give them a second thought because God, your God, is striding ahead of you. He's right there with you. He won't let you down; he won't leave you."

So then why, in the middle of our turmoil, does He *feel* so far away? Where has our focus been, you and me? Daily, we're bombarded with negative news as worry and disappointment constantly circle the track in our heads. Thus, we feel the familiar emotions of fear, insecurity, anxiety, and sadness.

It's not wrong to be sad. I get that. Terribly sad things are happening all around us, and grief is normal. Grief is necessary. Let yourself and your people grieve. But please, don't stay there. Let's turn our focus, turn our eyes, on our God. He's right here. Hold tightly to that truth.

A few years ago, our three-year-old grandson spent the night at our house. My husband woke to these sweet words whispered very quietly: "Gwandad, tan we pwease have some bweakfast?" When Grandad opened his eyes, the wee boy's face was hovering barely an inch above his own, nose to nose.

I think that's the way it is with God. Some people don't think He exists, and others think He is out there somewhere. But for those of us who have a relationship with Him, I want to remind you, God is right there, an inch from your nose. And in this we have hope and the promise of peace:

"May the God of hope fill you with all joy and peace as you trust in him, so that you may overflow with hope by the power of the Holy Spirit" (Rom. 15:13).

He hears you, night and day. He hears your anxious thoughts. He hears your fears, your sadness, your wonderings, and your doubts. And He cares. Talk to Him. Focus on Him.

Listen, Sister: I want to be filled with joy and peace, don't you? So, as we trust God, who has always been trustworthy, He will fill us with this joy and peace, even in the hardest, most confusing times. And, in turn, we will overflow with hope. And hope is exactly what all of us are looking for today.

Ducks in a Row

I squinted to see the fuzzy font inches from my face. Since when were words so blurry? *Old age is not my friend*, I thought as I leaned in closer to the computer screen. Straining hard, I tried to convince my eyes to focus, oblivious to the crystal-clear lesson I was about to learn.

The next morning, I applied a thick layer of foundation to my aging face as part of my hope-for-the-best morning routine. Perhaps the bottle of "light beige" would fill in the cracks and lines, magically wiping years off my appearance with the stroke of a brush like the Instagram-diva I adore.

But instead, glancing back at me, I noticed a peculiar cock-eyed smile. Something seemed odd; my face looked a bit off, and I hesitated. What was different? Smiling in the mirror, only half of my mouth lifted. I tried to wink, but I couldn't raise my right cheek. What the heck? My chest tightened as my brain buzzed with a myriad of possible diagnoses and the prospect of a future void of full-on smiles in hilarious situations.

Because I'm a logical person with a plate full of duties awaiting me, I drove straight to work. Ducks must be in a row, always. Obviously. Also, in my experience, busyness is a decent distraction when you're trying to avoid thinking about something serious—and I was.

A few hours—and a bazillion glances in the mirror later—my boss arrived at the office. Noticing my lop-sided smile, he voiced his concern, which sounded kind of pushy at the time, and demanded I go straight to the emergency room. God bless this man who was nothing but kind to me, always.

At the hospital, things started to ramp up. The emergency room lobby was piled high with folks anxious for help. I always find it interesting to see the cross-section of people in that waiting room. You can be a millionaire or a recipient of social assistance, but in that room, you are a number, and the number is likely a long one.

I learned a lot that day, starting with the fact that I likely should have gone a little earlier. Apparently, there is a small window of opportunity for a medication to be administered if someone has experienced a stroke. The silver lining, and you can always find one, Sister, is the expediated service granted to patients with my symptoms. It's like the fast pass at the amusement park—without the rides or the fun.

By the time my worried husband joined me in the curtain-walled examination room, my speech was garbled. Girlfriend, this sweet man is accustomed to strange and awkward things coming out of his wife's mouth, but this was a different type of disturbing experience.

"I don't understand!" I prayed.

I had been so confident that God was calling me to write and to speak to women. I knew He was telling me to share my story—or at least I thought I knew. Now, my mind reeled with doubt. My eyes were blurry, my words were slurred, and my confidence was shattered.

I knew nothing. Perhaps this was a sign, some cryptic demonstration from the Lord Himself advising me to throw in the towel. You know, like when someone offers you a decadent slice of caramel pecan cheesecake and you're sure it's a sign to kibosh the diet?

Have you ever been there? Have you been at a tough spot where you desperately want to give up? You reposition, get set, and try one more time, only to suffer another sucker punch to the gut. Have you been hitting roadblock after roadblock, wondering if maybe God is giving you access to the ejection button and hoping you have the good sense to pull it?

Wrapped in a stifling wet blanket of doubt and sadness, fear sold lies to my heart. And I bought them: *I can never do this. I have no talent, no ability, no education, and now blurred eyes and garbled speech. God knows I'm unable, and He's showing me the escape route. Run, Girl, run. Give up.*

In the quiet, in the darkness, I pled. I asked hard questions because, hey, God doesn't mind. He knows what I'm thinking anyway:

- God, is something happening to my brain? Am I having a stroke?
- Is my life changing for the worse now that I'm finally obeying you?
- Is this your way of telling me to quit?

Nothing. I heard nothing at that time except the beeps of testing machines and nurses rushing to and fro. I had no answer from God, no still small voice in the air vent, no revelation in my churning mind.

In the end, I didn't bail. Ricky prayed with and for me, and we moved forward one day at a time. And as I continued to do the next best step, we watched God do His thing. Because that's what all this is; this is His thing. It was never my thing in the first place. Job learned that lesson well:

> "I know that You can do all things, and that no purpose of Yours can be thwarted" (Job 42:2, NASB).

Girlfriend, God doesn't need us to do his bidding. He's not sitting, waiting for our obedience so He can finally go ahead with His plan. But God invites us into the story. He allows us and includes us. He lets us be a part so we can grow and learn and be blessed.

I find God reveals the plan to me one tiny piece at a time, one step of obedience at a time, which is good for me. He knows that's all I can handle. And He helps me keep those distracted ducks firmly in a row.

Listen, Sister: Do you sense God asking you to do something today? What is the next little step you can take?

Her Name Is Hannah

My husband affectionately refers to it as "the freakshow" when describing the state of pandemonium we experienced raising eight rambunctious boys into teenagers before our very eyes. He's thinking of all the toys, bikes, basketballs, and scooters that littered the yard. And believe me when I tell you, the laundry and dishes seemed never ending.

Absolutely everything was a competition at our house, from Marco Polo to Settlers of Catan, and the spacious kitchen floor hosted daily wrestling matches to solidify one's place in the teenage pecking order.

Amid the unending chaos, I had the brilliant idea that we needed a puppy. I'd like to pause right here and blame this notion on back-pain medication. Clearly, it's a decision I should have pondered for longer.

Hannah arrived on scene and fit right in, with her playful puppy attitude and love of games. If I could have looked ahead to see the kind of dog she would be, I likely would have named her Houdini or Frank Morris. Alas, we are not privy to such foresight.

Throughout her life, Hannah became well known for her ability to quietly weasel out of the house inconspicuously as a door hesitated to close or as she skillfully escaped our best attempts at backyard confinement.

One day, I returned home to a voicemail from the lady at the bank. A customer had reported a small dog walking alone down the middle of the road in our village. The dog was wearing a collar with a long chain trailing behind. Attached at the other end of the chain was a curly anchor stake, the kind you corkscrew into your lawn to detain your pet. Embarrassing? Wait, I'm not done yet.

Somehow caught up in the chain/spiral contraption were a G.I. Joe army jeep, various sandbox pails and shovels, and Cam's scooter. Hannah was proudly (and I suspect loudly) parading down the centre of the main street for all to see, dragging everything but the kitchen sink. It was quite a scene.

Maybe if she had worn a bright nametag that said, "Chriss Angel, escape artist," residents would have been more understanding.

Sometimes, I'm like Hannah. I try to lug around all the mistakes and bad choices I have made in the past. They're noisy and often distract me as they fill my thoughts. Believe me; that's a heavy, heavy chain to drag.

But that's not the truth. I'm thankful that God has His own names for us. He knows us intimately. He knows every thought I've ever had and everything I've ever done, yet He calls me His daughter. I love the sound of that name. Consider John 1:12:

"But as many as received him, to them gave he the right to become children of God, even to them that believe on his name" (NASB).

Listen, Sister: Your past doesn't determine who you are today. God says you are forgiven, and He chooses to forget your sin. He calls you daughter. So, why would *you* want to keep past mistakes in tow?

Fraud

I don't feel like it. I know I should pray. I know I should read my Bible. I should confide in my BFF. But I don't want to.

Lately, I've felt discouraged. If a friend confided in me, asking for advice to remedy her list of these common complaints and feelings, without a doubt, I know how I would respond. I'd say, "Change your thinking. Focus on truth. Ask God for help."

It's easy to tell other people what do. Encouraging women is kind of my jam. But when I'm pelted by the hailstones of discouragement, it's nearly impossible to listen to my own good advice.

So, then the enemy taunts me, firing sharp-edged accusations into the shadows. I think, *How dare I speak to my Sisters when my own mind is utter chaos? I am a mess. I'm a fraud. I'm disillusioned, incompetent, inadequate, and a loser.*

I'm called to cheer women on, and all the while, I sit staring at a blank page with absolutely no right to say a thing. I won't pretend I'm some kind of expert as I'm confronted with the same attacks we all face. Oppressive darkness envelopes me. I slump in defeat.

But slowly, one small, quiet thought seeps out through a crack. Two words: "Help me."

Relief is not immediate. No clouds part like an epic adventure movie; no dramatic film score plays in the background. No cool air floods the room, but a new thought comes: *request back up; join forces.*

Moment by moment, gaining sight, I recognize the attack for what it is. I remember the battle unseen by mortal eyes.

I love the visual of the ancient Roman armour. In battle, their oval shields could be linked together to create an impenetrable defensive barrier. What a great reminder to bind together, to pray for each other, and to stand firm.

Aren't we all fighting some sort of battle? We are fighting addiction, fighting cancer, fighting discouragement, fighting fear, and fighting lies.

What are you struggling with these days? Our lives are a constant fight. But know this: we don't fight alone. Let's click our shields together and form a solid defense against the enemy.

Remember the truth of who you are. If you have a relationship with Jesus, you are a daughter of the King! Talk to Him. He's always listening:

"I call on you, my God, for you will answer me; turn your ear to me and hear my prayer" (Ps. 17:6).

Let's be honest and transparent with our friends. Don't pretend to be "fine" when you really aren't. Let's hold one another up in prayer. Be there. Support each other in words and actions.

Trust that God is listening and ready to help. He's waiting for you. And rejoice in the clinking armour as we fight our battles together.

Listen, Sister: How about you? Who can you clink armour with to fight together today?

Fire in the Hole

There is nothing as wonderful as gathering the whole family under one roof. It's interconnected yet diverse pieces coming together to form one complete jigsaw puzzle in my heart. Grinning faces, tousled toe heads, and bro hugs mean love is pouring out all around. I love reliving the crazy antics of days gone by and , on one such day, creating a new story to add to the collection.

It was Easter weekend as one by one the families arrived to celebrate. Our kids have lots of people loving on them, and by the time it's our turn, they're usually sick and tired of turkey, ham, and other such customary offerings. I never mind breaking from tradition, thankfully avoiding the competition for the best bird or most famous dressing.

Here's a secret for you, Sister: I'm not a fabulous cook. OK, it's not really a secret. But my kids survived, and every one of them is strong and healthy by the grace of God and the blessing of Cheez Whiz. I'm calling that a win.

As the littles toddled downstairs to play, the grownups stood around the kitchen, chiding each other and soaking up the aroma of homemade lasagna in the oven behind me. I can usually be found backed up to the oven door because, well, heat is my friend.

Amid laughter and reminiscing, yet another childhood story was leaked; one I learned of only at that moment, twenty years after the fact. For this I am thankful. I'm sure I dodged innumerable grey hairs and a whole slew of forehead wrinkles by occasionally being allowed to live in oblivion.

As details were recalled, uproarious laughter filled the room. Tears streamed down my face, and I worked to dry my eyes and catch my breath, my stomach aching. Faintly, I remember hearing the word "fire," but to be honest, it didn't register in my brain. Laughter ensued as another brother added his detailed account of the shared memory.

The noise died down as the room fell strangely quiet. I glanced up as Jesse, the calm one, looked me straight in the eye and said, "Mom, there seems to be a fire in the oven."

It took a minute to register the frantic news, delivered in such a nonchalant tone: "It looks like rain. It appears your socks don't match. And there seems to be a fire in the oven."

I swung around, peering into the oven window. Girlfriend, why do they call that black square a window? Is it ever clean enough to look through? But it was easy to see there were indeed wild flames dancing right behind me.

The lasagna! I hesitated, pausing momentarily. I was a bit fearful of opening the door and providing more oxygen to this blaze, mostly because of the movie *Backdraft*, which I had watched the trailer for years ago. Also, I was working at the fire school at the time. This ruled out any plan to call for professional help as that would kindle incessant teasing that would most definitely follow me all the days of my life.

On the other hand, twenty people were hoping to eat lasagna, so a girl's gotta do what a girl's gotta do.

We pulled the pan out, extinguished the fire, and squelched the smoke alarms, debating how a tin foil pan of pasta could cause an infernal blaze to fill the old appliance.

The air reeked of melted plastic, but eventually the room cleared, leaving only a bucketful of questions. Upon further investigation, we noticed long, thick drips of plastic from the oven rack down to the element, like stalactites in a hidden cave. How bizarre.

Thinking through the Easter dinner prep, I recalled making the lasagna a few days prior and freezing it, wrapping the tin foil pan in aluminum foil. But the new foil pan came with a handy dandy plastic lid. Not wanting to be wasteful, I tucked the useless lid under the pan and plopped the whole thing in the freezer, and subsequently in the oven. Although now, there was no plastic lid to be found.

Well, I did find the lid I suppose, dripping down and flaming high, creating yet another family story and filling us with laughter. What a gift! Job 8:21 says,

"He will yet fill your mouth with laughter and your lips with shouts of joy."

Listen, Sister: Laughter is truly good for the soul. It bonds us together and eliminates stress. And if we need to have a major kitchen blunder to bring this kind of joy to our family, well, so be it. I can be that kind of mom.

Finding Purpose

As the years take flight before my very eyes, I often reflect on things I've heard as a young girl. My grama would regularly tell me the days pass quickly; at the time, I couldn't wait for Friday, let alone Christmas or adulthood. And here I am, Grami myself, passing on these pearls of wisdom to my granddaughters as they look away and roll their eyes. Gazing in the rear-view mirror, I'm reminded that, despite the stage of womanhood we're in, God has a calling for us, perfect at just that juncture.

Some of us are moms of little ones, changing bums and longing for five minutes of time to ourselves.

Some are bringing up teenagers. These precious parents are hanging on, white-knuckled, to life on a hormone-driven rollercoaster.

Others have spent long years raising their kids into adults and now dwell in often tidier and much quieter homes.

Most of all, I've been thinking of those who have not worn the "Mother" nametag but still long for it. Countless women ache for motherhood with fractured hearts as they anxiously watch months pass by them again and again.

Let me tell you about just such a woman, one whom I deeply admire. She grew up with the life goal of being a wife and mother, and if the appointment of "Mom" was based on credentials, she would have it hands down. She has every quality a good mother possesses. But she has yet to officially become one.

It's been a puzzling, heartsick journey for her, and I've watched with absolute respect as this young lady has been an incredible example to me. You see, she doesn't spend her days pining for what she doesn't have. Instead, she pours her entire life into other people, especially children. She delights in and cheers on her friends' kids. She's an official Big Sister, volunteering through the Big Brothers Big Sisters youth mentoring program, and has fed into the lives of Little Sisters in the most loving and doggedly consistent way for years. As a foster parent, she makes immense sacrifices daily. My friend has forever changed the trajectory of the lives of a whole slew of children. This woman is an amazing "mom" in so many ways.

No matter what stage of life we're at, it is common to search for purpose. We can be disillusioned when we think we know what we need but God isn't giving it to us.

Or maybe we were on a roll raising kids, but now they've moved out. There were times (mainly in the teen years) we begged God for this day, but now the nest is empty, and we're searching for direction.

Girlfriend, God has a purpose for you right where you are today. It may not look like what you thought it would. It may not be what you would pick, given the choice. Take a step back, change your focus, and watch for ways to serve others. There are lots of opportunities that fit your distinct gifts and personality. Start with something small; ask God for guidance.

Isaiah wrote this to encourage the hearts of women, despite their official motherhood status.

"'Sing, O barren woman, you who never bore a child; burst into song, shout for joy, you who were never in labor; because more are the children of the desolate woman than of her who has a husband,' says the LORD" (Is. 54:1).

Listen, Sister: If we intentionally think outside of ourselves, we can enrich the lives of others and find purpose right where we are today.

Ashes to Ashes

There's nothing as appreciated as a cool breeze on a sweltering day—unless you're moving ashes.

Our big, old family farmhouse rested in the shade of a mighty maple. In the summer months, the windows were propped wide, pleading for any sort of airflow, but when the bitter winds drove drifts of snow across the open fields, the wood-burning furnace filled the rooms with smoky, warm heat morning till night.

Wood is cost-effective, and I loved hunkering down in the winter being kept warm by a roaring fire, but temperature control was a bit tricky.

On the coldest nights of the year, with the wind howling at the windows, I'd lay on my bed, sweating in my baby doll pyjamas, only to wake up as an ice block when the fire went out before morning.

As I remember, the only daughter in our family was assigned most of the chores growing up. My brothers did do some tasks outside, likely, I think. One of their chores was to clean the ashes out of the furnace. This required a steady hand and intense concentration. One jolt, one gust of wind, and the ash would scatter everywhere. Have you ever seen ashes blowing around, maybe from an extinguished campfire or an unfortunate incident in your oven? Good luck gathering those up again.

I like to think of my past this way. All the awful things I've done, the horrible choices that brought heartache to myself and the people I love, those are forgiven. God says that once we're forgiven, our sin is no more. It's like ashes in the wind.

It's only the enemy who reminds us of our failures. He plants seeds of doubt and feelings of shame and guilt in our heads. His game plan is always to jam us up, to make us less effective, and ultimately to distract us from our new life of freedom.

But this is what I've learned to be true: God paid for my sin with His blood, and then He "burned it up." It's no more. It's ashes. You can't take a handful of ashes and determine what the log looked like. It's impossible, isn't it?

So, why do I get sucked into this lousy trip down the pathway where guilt meets shame? Oh, the devil is tricky. But, Girlfriend, we have truth. When we confess and ask God for forgiveness, our sin becomes ashes, burned up, forgotten. And we are set free, no longer attached to a life of guilt.

And God promises to take the black, charred remains of our old lives and transform them into something beautiful. I'd say that's a great trade. We are promised this renewal several times in the Word:

- "I, even I, am he who blots out your transgressions, for my own sake, and remembers your sins no more" (Is. 43:25).
- "As far as the east is from the west, so far has he removed our transgressions from us" (Ps. 103:12).

Listen, Sister: When we hand our bucket of ashes to God, He has something spectacular in mind for us.

Made for a Purpose

What if I told you that a one-hundred-year-old rooster gave me food for thought this week?

As a little girl, spending days with my Grama was the best thing ever. With nothing but time on our hands, we huddled close, sipping warm tea while singing along to old records or watching Bob Barker give away prizes on the big console TV.

Our meals were simple and yummy, and finishing my plate was never the pre-requisite for enjoying dessert: soft oatmeal cookies and fresh fruit, covered in cool cream. I can almost taste it today.

Grama poured cream from a hand-painted rustic rooster. He was unlike any pitcher you've used in your home. At least, I imagine this to be true. His paint was worn and his beak chipped, but I thought him to be stately and magnificent.

The noble rooster was originally owned by my great-grandmother Belle and reportedly served cream fresh from the cow's udder.

When I asked Grama why this precious heirloom wasn't resting in the china cabinet, she answered matter-of-factly, "He was made for a purpose."

Never mind the scrapes, the chips, the hairline cracks. This pitcher was made to be used.

Today, as I glance over at this rooster, retired to my shelf, it gives me hope. I'm reminded that despite my age, my struggles, my mistakes, and past failures, God still intends to use me.

But wait. Maybe I'm a prime candidate for service not *despite* my cracks but *because of* my flaws. I am well acquainted with weakness. I realize that when God calls me to something, there is no chance I can do it in my own power. But I have God's power shining through my cracks.

Do you ever feel like my rooster? Worn? Faded? Used? Me too! Sin from my past (long forgiven) weighs heavy on my heart. I'm certain the big mistakes I made will disqualify me from anything good in the future. I've screwed up way too many times. I wonder if God only uses the "good girls" in his great plans. And, Girlfriend, if this is true, I would *not* make the cut. But it is not true.

Tell God today that your heart is willing. Get ready for opportunities to love people. And be warned; it will look entirely different than you expect. But rest assured; it's going to be an amazing adventure. He is waiting for you, just the way you are, cracks and all:

"But we have this treasure in jars of clay to show that this all-surpassing power is from God and not from us" (2 Cor. 4:7).

Listen, Sister: God, who moulded us into being with His own hands, chooses to forgive. He loves us despite all of it and invites us into His big adventure. The only requirement is a willing heart. Isn't this amazing news?

Desperate to Escape

C ountry living is a lot like growing up in the city. Although our surroundings contrasted sharply, danger still lurks around the corner—or across the field, as the case may be.

Instead of a fenced yard, manicured lawn, and smooth cement perfect for training wheels, my brothers and I grew up with tall grass, dusty gravel, and wide-open spaces. Bawling calves replaced sirens and horns, and the only air pollution was the odour wafting in from the hog farm down the dirt road. We lived in the boonies, you could say.

There was no "stranger danger" on our farm, and the concept of parents entertaining children had yet to be invented. We made our own fun, and our world seemed limitless, as long as we didn't venture past the sentinel post, midway down the pine-lined laneway.

I remember one drizzly day when we decided to take a shortcut through a plowed field. Jack and I were just little guys, clad in mismatched clothes and rubber boots past our knees. But reaching the halfway point in our trek, the ground turned to marshy gunk beneath our feet. With each step, our legs became heavier, the wet clay fighting, reluctant to release our feet. And then, abruptly we stopped. We were trapped, prisoners of the mud.

As the ever-responsible sister, I tried to pull my little brother up, out of the muck, but to no avail. Yep, we were stuck. So, we did the only thing we could do. We held hands and cried out for help. We could do nothing else. At the end of our pitiful selves, in desperation, we raised our voices in a unified wail.

Now and then, I still feel like that little girl. Stuck. Stuck in the anguish. Stuck in the unbearable. Sinking in quicksand, paralyzed, powerless to change my situation. I feel unable to move, to breathe.

In my six-year-old brain, Jack and I were stranded and hopeless in the wet cropland for roughly one thousand hours before our mother came to rescue us. I bet in her perspective it wasn't that long at all. But perspective is hard to come by when you're mid-thigh in wet clay.

Girlfriend, let's take a lesson today from the little ones. As babies, you and I knew instinctively to cry for help. We recognized our dependence on our parents. Our weakness wasn't embarrassing or humiliating. Naturally, we cried out for rescue.

Are you struggling today, stuck, desperate to escape? Is your mind racing endlessly, exhausted, desperate for freedom?

Cry out, my friend. Cry out to God with every fiber of your being as Romans 8:25 describes:

"Likewise the Spirit helps us in our weakness. For we do not know what to pray for as we ought, but the Spirit himself intercedes for us with groanings too deep for words."

He knows your situation well. If you don't know Him personally, He is pursuing you right now. He wants an intimate relationship with you. He longs to comfort you and give you peace.

Listen, Sister: Let's join hands and cry out. Let's raise our voices together in a collective wail. And if you don't have anyone praying alongside you, let me know. I will be happy to hold that spot.

Dummyhead

Raising a family bursting with boys has been many things, but boring is not one of them. With the middle ranks of our blended family boasting five boys in a four-year age range, there was never a dull moment. Wrestling matches, board games, sports teams, and full-out elastic wars were the call of the day. But life wasn't always coming up roses, that's for sure.

For the most part, this band of brothers got along famously. But as with all families, inevitably, disputes would crop up, resulting in some pretty nasty name calling. Dummyhead, loser, and, to be honest, other much more flowery descriptors were shot around like well-aimed hockey pucks on a continual basis.

To alleviate this constant barrage of name calling, and since simple appeals for kindness or silence were not heeded, we implemented a plan. We called it the "Three Nice Things Rule."

The premise was simple. If you said something mean about someone, you must immediately follow up with three nice things.

Believe me when I tell you that nobody wants to do this. Your brother, hot and frustrated, feeling justified in his anger and spewing names like sharp stones from a slingshot, is in no way inspired to speak life-giving words in the next breath. Yet they had to. It was terrific.

Words are powerful. They can build us up, encourage, and inspire us, or they can devastate, dismay, and knock the wind out of our sails.

Research shows it takes five to seven positive comments just to balance out one negative. It's no wonder our kids sometimes grow up insecure and discouraged. And it's not just children who need kind words. I do, and I bet you do too.

Words spoken tend to stick with us for years to come. They can shape what we think about ourselves and even change our trajectory in life. Often, we recall a negative comment many years later. Likewise, words of encouragement can also change someone's day, give them life, and inspire them to carry on.

I will never forget a lazy spring day over forty years ago. Gravel crunched beneath my feet, and the smell of country living filled the air as I sauntered down the long farm laneway to the mailbox with my dad. On that day, seemingly out of nowhere, my father told me he was proud of me. It had nothing to do with academics, acquired height, or musical ability—that much is for sure. I guess I didn't ask why. I just basked in the thought. That awkward fourteen-year-old girl, who was struggling to fit in, failing to measure up, and searching for love and purpose, gripped those words like a life preserver thrown to a drowning swimmer. My dad was proud of me.

There are moments even now that I close my eyes and return to that stone laneway and the shade of the big maple tree just to hear those words again.

These are the type of words I long to give to my people, to my children, my husband, and my friends. Don't you? Let's encourage each other at every opportunity:

"Therefore encourage one another and build each other up, just as in fact you are doing" (1 Thess. 5:11).

Listen, Sister: Look around, watch for opportunities, and intentionally encourage someone today.

Feeling Isolated

Lately, I've been learning the difference between introverts and extro-verts—but not through your run-of-the-mill online course. Rather, I've been learning through life *chez* Scott.

One of us here is definitely an extrovert. She is a lover of people, of connecting, of light-hearted banter, and a big fan of loud Rummoli nights with the girls. She is crazy about her humungous family, passionate for com-petitive board games, and deeply desires long, tight hugs.

In the other corner, we have the introvert. I'm learning that he draws energy from just being alone. He needs a lot of time to ponder deeply before responding, prefers to be uninterrupted in the morning, and although he misses family, he seems to be coping just fine in this quiet house.

Confession: I'm finding time alone to be incredibly lonely. As our lives change through the different seasons and stages of life, we're forced to figure out our new normal. Are you feeling it these days too? The weeks drag on, and Fridays and Tuesdays are sometimes indistinguishable.

Today I can joke about it, but yesterday my throat singed hot as I fought back tears. My husband left for work, and my son is on some kind of a "mid-afternoon is the new morning" schedule. Even then, I'm far from a desirable companion for a sixteen-year-old who has an entourage of cool friends literally at his fingertips. So, there I sat, alone and discouraged.

I feel deserted by all my friends as our lives morph and drift in unexpected directions. I'm worried they will move on without me, too busy to connect.

How do you and I beat this looming loneliness? I know the standard (and true) Jesus-girl answer: lean into God. But seriously, what does that even mean? When I can't see Jesus in the flesh, how can I snuggle in for that big bear hug I so desperately need?

Well, I know what leaning into Him does *not* mean:

- Binge-watching seasons of shows on Netflix
- Yet another glass of wine to mask the heartache
- A pity party listing all the people I miss but can't invite to this lonely assembly of one

We recognize our thoughts lead to our emotions. So, let's change our thoughts. Yesterday I forced myself to make a new list, though I honestly didn't *feel* like doing this at all. Just try it.

Things for which I am thankful:

- Wildflowers poking up through the grass
- The smell of hotdogs broiling on the barbecue
- Bright red cardinals chattering in the bush outside my window

And girlfriend, I have been here in this desolate place before, so I know that making this list every day changes my heart. Thankfulness reminds my soul that God is blessing me. And He brings joy amid isolation:

"In every situation [no matter what the circumstances] be thankful *and* continually give thanks *to God*; for this is the will of God for you in Christ Jesus" (1 Thess. 5:18, AMP).

Listen, Sister: When you are down, when your chest is burning with anxiety and you can't shake the fear crushing in on you, make a mental list. Think of three gifts you've received and thank God for them today.

A Sight for Sore Eyes

There are clearly defined signs of aging, and let me tell you, I am living every one of them.

My friends barely finished the well-harmonized chorus of "Happy Birthday" when my body took the cue and went into full revolt. From the bunions on my toes to my ever-expanding waistline, middle age is an unwanted adventure in reconstruction. Just wait, Sister, if you're chuckling to yourself as you look at your firm skin and slender physique; your turn is coming.

Lately, I've had a problem with my eyesight. Initially, I was in denial; surely not another body part had enlisted in the mutiny. And then the other day, I walked right past one of my best girlfriends. I mean, I did see something there, but she was blurry, and I couldn't be sure.

Listen, Sister, I would never walk right past you. I live to connect and gab and catch up and hug. So, there you have it; something had to be done.

Choosing eyewear is almost the worst thing ever. Apparently, if you want to see the highway, your computer screen, and your hand in front of your eyes, that is called "multiple fields of vision." I won't go further into all the technical stuff, but here's the gist: the eyeglass prescription of a woman over forty requires more acreage than what will fit on the lens of those trendy slender frames.

And shopping for frames is like grocery shopping with twin toddlers. I'd rather clean the bathroom in a house full of little boys.

At times I've dragged Ricky along with me because every relationship flourishes in settings where one person is close to losing her mind in frustration and the other is too afraid to give his honest opinion. On other occasions, I've begged the store attendant to quickly pick something so I could be done with it. I'm pathetic.

So, I was eager to finally pick up my new glasses and looking forward to the gift of clear sight again, if only for the sake of other motorists. I was also pretty proud of my bold decision to choose navy blue over brown frames. What a rebel.

But within a day or two, a dull chisel began to persistently chip away the front of my brain, and each evening I wanted to claw my eyes right out of my face. Yet my vision was clear. I could have read just fine—if I didn't need to sit in a dark room with my eyes closed because of the pain. Counterproductive.

My husband "encouraged" me to return to the eyeglass store, and as it turned out, he was right. The prescription was wrong. I don't understand optometry, but I recall hearing words like "one number off," "astigmatism," and other scientific terms. My lens was wrong, and I didn't even know.

We all view the world through our individual lens, don't we? Our life experiences, our heart, and our focus all put a spin on every situation we see. One person sees an addict, allowing the struggle to define the individual; another, who has perhaps walked the agonizing road of recovery with their own sweet son, sees that same man as a precious child aching to be set free from the tenacious tentacles of bondage.

Yet God sees all of us through His lens of perfect love. Aren't you thankful? He knows our story. He knows our past, our struggles, and our deepest secrets. He knows the atrocities that torture us, even if we've never told a living soul. And He understands the deepest longings of our heart.

It's through this lens that He sees us. It's the lens of sacrificial love, a love that led Him to trade His life for me and for you. I'm so thankful He sees me today.

"She gave this name to the LORD who spoke to her: 'You are the God who sees me,' for she said, 'I have now seen the One who sees me'" (Gen. 16:13).

Listen, Sister: Let's ask God to give us His lens, to grant us the capacity to see others as He does. Oh, the freedom we could all enjoy if we were truly seen and understood.

I'm certain that God sees me as I truly am. He doesn't see a middle-aged lady whose body is in full revolt, but instead, He sees His daughter, a woman after His own heart.

Curbside Delivery

My husband, Ricky, is one in a million. He's kind, generous, and patient, which is of utmost importance considering his wife. He's a solid type two on the Enneagram, meaning he subconsciously spends his time on the lookout for ways to serve others. When this naturally applies to me, all the better. Over the years, we've grown in our relationship with each other and with God, and I couldn't love him more. I've actually married him twice.

Of course, our second wedding was a low-key event—no long, white dress, calla lily bouquet, or decorated table heaped with wedding gifts. That's too bad because I really could've used new sheets.

In the time when bed sheets and underwear were deemed non-essential by the government, things got crazy. What type of country could decide haircuts, restaurants, and birthday balloons were unlawful and promote alcohol, cigarettes, and recreational marijuana? O, Canada. Lord, have mercy on us all.

Seeing the next-door neighbours whisper and point as I once again hung our thread-bare sheets on the clothesline, it was time to give in and spring for a new set. Also, my entire hand had been stuck in a hole all night, causing me to wake up in a full-on sweat, feeling trapped and claustrophobic. The insanity had to end.

Ordered online and paid for, the brand-new sheets were ready to be picked up curbside, and my anticipation was mounting. New sheets! These are the things you look forward to in your fifties, sweet Sister, the excitement of new sheets.

My husband was getting groceries (bless this man), and knowing my parcel was ready at a store in the same plaza, he readily offered to pick it up. See? He's wonderful. Also, he was sick and tired of his toes getting caught in his own little hole in the sheet.

The department store is situated under a massive colourful sign, and as Ricky headed in that direction, he noticed a homeless guy sitting on the curb. His clothes were dirty and tattered, and his shaky hand lifted a wine bottle to his lips. As he took a swig, staring nowhere in particular, the overwhelming odour of pot filled the air, assaulting the senses. The man looked up and away, unconcerned with any retribution from this off-duty drug enforcement officer.

Finally reaching the front of the line, my husband requested the parcel from the clerk at the doorway pick-up station.

"For Tess Scott," he explained.

Finding no parcel and nothing in the system, they spelled my name various ways, including "Teresa," which is the name my mother uses when I'm getting heck. Still no sign of my order.

Citing the order number and with the assistance of the store manager, there was still no luck, and my usually calm husband was beginning to get a tiny bit frustrated.

"I have the confirmation email right here."

He handed his phone over to the attendant as proof positive. Reading the email, a huge grin spread across the clerk's face.

"You're going to find this funny," the clerk promised. "You're at the cannabis store. The department store is next door, and their curbside pick-up is around back."

So let me repeat: marijuana out front; sheets in the alley. Sometimes you just have to laugh.

> "A happy heart makes the face cheerful, but heartache crushes the spirit" (Prov. 15:13).

Listen, Sister: Take a step back and smile. Life can be a roller-coaster ride, and deciding to laugh at yourself is one way to bring joy to your heart and to the people around you. Share something funny today.

Buckle Up

I remember a time long ago when I was a perky little waitress slinging burgers at a roadside diner, oblivious to danger right around the corner. The kitschy little eatery doubled as a landing strip and hosted a string of airplane hangars with "fly-ins" every weekend.

We served simple food in a down-home atmosphere. Locals would pull up a chair to join any table in progress and share the neighbourhood gossip or promise of rain on the thirsty bean fields.

Chiding each other and teasing the staff, all sorts of small-town characters came together daily for a decent meal and good fun.

I remember a bunch of Levi-clad farmers, doubling as pilots, egging me on to venture up in a plane one sunny Saturday. The sky was clear, and after a bit of protesting, I finally caved in. Before I knew it, I was buckled into the tiny aircraft and leaving the ground on an exciting voyage.

As the plane left the runway, I quickly learned the difference between take-off in a Boeing jet and lifting off while harnessed to the seat of a flimsy tin can, careening toward the sky.

Simultaneously, I was reminded of both my fear of heights and my propensity for motion sickness. A blazing inferno erupted in my chest and pumped through my veins at lightning speed. Channels of sweat poured from my face. Knuckles white and clenched in terror, I closed my eyes.

What if we crash? How will they identify my body? Oh, my word, I'm going to puke.

Swallowing hard as saliva flooded my mouth, I peeked ever so slightly in search of a can, a box, a bag, or any sort of receptacle. Suddenly, the bottom dropped out, and the plane plummeted as the pilot chuckled at my expense.

Eventually, we leveled out above the clouds, and I opened my eyes to exquisite beauty beyond measure. The sky was tranquil, serene, and breathtaking as I stared in awe.

Sometimes the road to beautiful is bumpy. It's scary. There is no roadmap, and the path seems uncertain at best. We white-knuckle it, peering around for a parachute.

But when I was airborne all those years ago in that metal death trap, in the scared-stiff, panic-stricken moments, do you know what I *didn't* do? I didn't reach over and take the controls. You see, my pilot was experienced. He had a pilot license, and his grey hair spoke of hundreds of successful flights.

Girlfriend, how much more will we trust the One who holds all of it in His hands? I'm not saying this is easy. Often, our hearts ache for a glimpse of a bright tomorrow, an inkling of when the agony will end, or a reminder that there is joy to be found during trouble.

And someday, we will open our eyes to the most radiant, magnificent sight.

"For I reckon that the sufferings of this present time are not worthy to be compared with the glory which shall be revealed in us" (Rom. 8:18, ASV).

Listen, Sister: For now, we live one step at a time, one day at a time. And the One who holds me and holds you, the One we can run to and who is always faithful, calls us to an awesome life of adventure. So, buckle up, Sister.

Cooties

think I know how Carol felt in grade one. She had cooties. The moment her shabby, too tight running shoes hit the tarmac, the entire population of primary students abandoned their playground activities and rushed away like a herd of antelopes running for their lives as a hungry lion appeared on the horizon. Only Carol wasn't a lion. She was a poor, sweet child. I cannot imagine her confusion and sadness as, day after day, her wee heart faced rejection and ridicule. I didn't consider that at the time. I was five.

One day, in the thick of the pandemic, I was walking down the sidewalk enjoying the scent of freshly cut grass, and I spotted a man mowing the boulevard. As I approached, he let go of his lawnmower and (to protect himself from me) moved onto the road, affording me a wide berth as I passed.

The bitter sting of rejection slapped me in the face. I was shocked. I wasn't coughing, had recently showered—I took a quick account of this in my head to make sure—and I did not have cooties. But then, neither did Carol.

That familiar sense of rejection cropped up in my brain often in the days of the pandemic. Folks crossed the street to pass each other, and even close friends felt the need to keep their social distance. Strangers were quick to display their disapproval of others' choices, and if you accidentally found yourself walking the wrong way down the store aisle (there were arrows?), you were sure to receive some nasty glances.

In a 2010 study called "Humans Are Hardwired for Connection" (https://www.wcwonline.org/2010/humans-are-hardwired-for-connection-neurobiology-101-for-parents-educators-practitioners-and-the-general-public), researchers found the area that lit up in the brain as a result of social rejection—the anterior cingulate—was the exact same area that lights up for the distress of physical pain. Dr. Amy Banks pointed out that the distress of social pain is biologically identical to the distress of physical pain.

This is hard stuff. The pain of rejection is real. Can you relate?

Here is what we need to remember. These actions, reactions, or choices are not directed at us. We have no way of knowing the story of other people, and they don't always know ours. I have friends who have lost loved ones to the COVID-19 virus and are forced to grieve without family huddled around. Others are enduring chemo treatments along with a host of other vulnerabilities. Some have autistic kids, and this total break from routine is debilitating at best. Some people are living with a spouse who hates them, and the constant conflict at home is beyond belief. And to top it all off, we must consider mental health. Depression and fear are huge issues, and we have barely begun to see the devastating effects of this.

Instead of taking this rejection personally, being offended and holding this inside, let's decide to let it go. I will give up my little pity party.

These are difficult times indeed for every single one of us in different ways. We all want things to return to normal. We want to hug our grandkids, and you want to send your children back to school.

But until then, I am going to support other people. If they make different choices than I would, I want to accept that, not take it personally. Let's remember that each of us is making our best choice with our unique situation. Let's respond as Christ followers:

"Therefore, as God's chosen people, holy and dearly loved, clothe yourselves with compassion, kindness, humility, gentleness and patience" (Col. 3:12).

Listen, Sister: You *can* control your thinking, which will change how you feel. You can choose a different thought. Every single time you feel rejected, stop and remember that Jesus Himself was rejected as He walked this earth, and, in turn, He promises to never reject you.

Showering is still advisable.

Becoming a Pilot

There were always loads of work to be done on the farm, no matter the season. I'm sure you're not surprised to learn that us kids weren't always keen on helping. On occasion, when we were forced to lend a hand, I remember my dad comparing us to teats on a boar. If you're a city slicker, understand this is not a positive thing. But such is the life of a father.

Realizing the necessity of teaching his children the importance of work, Dad turned to creative ways to enlist our help.

Once, he told us to invite all the neighbour kids to our house on Saturday for a "rock concert." This was confusing to me. As far as I knew, he was more of a country and western type of guy. But, alas, I was young and optimistic, so I kept my fingers crossed.

The rock concert was, in fact, a day of stone picking. Trudging for hours in the blazing sun, up and down the field behind a tractor, we lifted giant rocks and hoisted them up into the wagon. This was even less fun than you might imagine and left our friends suspicious of all future invitations.

I remember my excitement the day my dad promised to teach me to be a pilot. Obviously, I wasn't very old at the time because it didn't occur to me that we didn't have a runway or even a plane for that matter.

I trusted him and listened carefully as he told me to bundle up and follow him through the snow to the woods behind our house.

Disappointingly, he taught me to "pile it"—not to become a pilot—and as I stacked firewood for the furnace, I was grateful for the extra layers of clothing the sly man had suggested.

While my dad had a plan for that day, our heavenly Father has a good plan for our entire future. He's put a calling on our lives that accounts for every gift, every talent, and every interest that we harbour. He uses our experiences and the person they've woven us into for His glory.

He even foresaw our foolishness and took all of it into account in His grand scheme. Sister, I'm extremely thankful for this very thing.

We don't have to rack our brains to figure out what God has for us. He's revealing it, stage by stage, day by day. Girlfriend, are you a "big picture" kind of girl like I am? I want to see the end game. I wonder, *How will this turn out? What will it look like? What's the big plan?* But lately I've been noticing that God isn't letting me see it this way. He's asking me to engage with Him every day and simply do the next thing, to trust He has plans for my life:

"For I know the plans I have for you," declares the Lord, "plans to prosper you and not to harm you, plans to give you hope and a future" (Jer. 29:11).

Listen, Sister: God is inviting us, including us, and preparing us (bundle up) for something marvelous. We need to tune in, be available, ask for opportunities, and follow one step at a time— even if we don't understand the reason, even if we don't think we can do it, and even if we can't see the plane.

Boat Builder

We grew up with dusty gravel roads, towering rows of corn, and the serenade of tree frogs filling the fresh air. Morning dawned with bawling calves and the fragrant scent of lilacs below my bedroom window. My best friend was my little brother—he had no choice since I was the boss—but that friendship didn't last long.

We made our own fun on the farm in those days, and our imaginations knew no end. A random collection of wood sat abandoned alongside the hen house. It was composed of decaying planks and shingles, all well-weathered, twisted, and cracked—a bunch of junk to the untrained eye. Jack wanted to build a boat, and I could help. But there was a challenge. We were not allowed to use nails. Or screws. Or saws. So basically, we had a bunch of planks.

Day after day, for hours on end, my brother sorted and planned and figured how we could make a boat. He did not give up. If that pile remained there today, I'm convinced he might still be working on it. His perseverance is phenomenal.

Time marched on, and we grew as children do. One of us became a miserable teenage girl. The other suffered through it. To say that I treated my brother horribly would be a great understatement. Using the excuse of his geekiness, a legitimate claim at the time, I ignored him and consistently disowned him in front of my friends. I cringe at the thought of it. Jack returned my harsh treatment with kindness, time and time again, and persevered in his quest to maintain a relationship with me.

Now, we have families of our own, and I moved around the corner to live closer to him. Who would have thought? We have a rock-solid connection, and I am forever thankful. My brother taught me the value of relationships; he taught me not to give up and to persevere. He also taught me forgiveness. My past offenses have no part in our relationship today because he has chosen to forgive me. We've moved on.

Are you holding on to an offense from the past? Is it affecting a relationship?

Girlfriend, I find myself trapped on this side of the fence sometimes too, holding grudges for transgressions long past. We must let go, forgive, and move on. After all, isn't that what we desire from others? Remember Matthew 6:14:

"For if you forgive other people when they sin against you, your heavenly Father will also forgive you."

Jack is a great example of Christ's love for me. God's forgiveness means that my offense is wiped away and my relationship is restored. What a gift! I'm thankful for my brother who has taught me many things in life, and it all started with building a boat.

Listen, Sister: Is there someone in your life that you are holding in unforgiveness? Why not ask God to help you with this today?

Dig It Up

We blended our family in a big, old four-bedroom fixer-upper. Blending families is a cutesy way of saying I had kids, he had kids, and we hoped for the best as we added one more to round things out.

Family life and home renovations are both stress-inducing endeavours, and attempting these simultaneously proved to be an ambitious and eventful season.

The previous owners of our new home had converted part of the back lawn to an enormous dog run. They took the fence with them when they moved, leaving solid clay and bark chips to cover the ground. This was prime "little boy" real estate, and our first priority was to plant grass.

The land was rock hard, and try as he did, with sweat gushing, my hubby could not penetrate the surface with a shovel. We needed a rototiller.

Enter my dad. Dad was one of the most generous people you'd ever want to meet. Hearing of our trouble, he offered the use of his rototiller and even his pick-up truck to transport it. "That'll do the trick," he promised with a wink.

Arriving at the farm, we found the rusty, old implement out behind the barn, hidden in tall grass and leaning hard on a fence post. This was not a promising sign. Straining in the blazing sun to budge it free from overgrown weeds and dislodge the metal tines from the rock-like field, sweat-soaked my man's shirt and did nothing for his mood.

I've learned the hard way to limit conversations with my husband at times like this. Sister, if you have a good idea, even if you know a better way to do something, for the love of all things peaceful, do not mention it. Just. Don't.

Finally wedging the rototiller free, my sweaty husband climbed into Dad's truck to bring it around and load the machine up. At that very moment, he noticed one of the truck tires was soft, bordering on completely flat. Since Ricky is a city slicker and not accustomed to the "it'll be fine" mantra of backwoods life, he felt the need to fix the tire before loading could begin. A frustrating affair beginning with a quest for tools and ending in yet more perspiration.

Eventually, we got the thing loaded and started off for home, when we noticed the gas gauge needle peeking out just below *E*. Rerouting to the nearest town, we prayed hard for a miracle and watched as God brought us all the way to the gas pump on nothing but fumes. He is good.

Finally home and unloaded, I watched my husband, strong and determined, as he glanced back at me, raising his eyebrows with a shrug. It had been quite a day. Reaching for the rototiller pull cord, he grabbed the handle and gave it a good rip. The entire rotten cord dissolved, leaving the handle alone in his hand.

What an exercise in futility. From start to finish, warning signs, roadblocks, and delays filled the entire day.

Do you have days like this? I do. And if we're willing, we can learn important things right in the moment. Here are my main take-aways from that day long ago:

- When your partner is sweating profusely, do not point out the obvious.
- Never compare your husband and your dad in your husband's presence.
- Even when you are right, don't mention it.
- Now is never the time for Pollyanna.

We've now developed a system over here. My husband does the heavy lifting, and I ride along to lift his spirits. I've learned that understanding and encouragement go a long way in the face of adversity. He always appreciates my support but also prefers the non-verbal type of cheerleading. I'm a work in progress.

We all appreciate encouragement. Remember what Paul says in his first letter to the Corinthians when they were experiencing loads of trouble.

"Who comforts us in all our troubles, so that we can comfort those in any trouble with the comfort we ourselves receive from God" (2 Cor. 1:4).

Listen, Sister: Working together on the rocky road of life can cement our relationships if we let it. It's not easy, but with God's help we can encourage each other and dig down for an even deeper relationship.

Concealed

efore I put my feet on the bedroom floor, I had a hunch it wasn't going to be an ordinary day. The fleeting thought momentarily touched down, teasing my crowded mind as I hurried to get ready for work.

I had woken with a start, unable to breathe. My nose was blocked, barricading any attempt at airflow, and a full-blown sinus headache lingered at the fringe of my subconscious, pacing, antsy, waiting its turn to occupy my clogged head.

Rooting through the bathroom closet I found it, the Vicks VapoRub. Is it just me, or were you raised on this stuff too, Sister?

My grama was the number one fan of this magical ointment; it was her go-to answer to any and every ailment. When my firstborn fell off his tricycle and scraped his knee badly, she lathered his bloody wound with an ample supply. I could imagine the horror he experienced as Grama later reported applying this sure-fire remedy while he screamed bloody murder. I bet he did!

So, to be clear, I don't recommend this treatment for scrapes and cuts, but a smidgen in the edge of your nostril will clear those airways lickety-split.

With a small dab inserted, I continued my morning routine, grabbing coffee and returning to the bathroom to "put my face on."

211

The makeup concealer (aka, friend of those of us with age spots) spread easily, and I remember thinking, as I went about my day, that my skin looked smoother than ever before.

Hours later, sitting at my desk, I rubbed my eye. Immediately tears gushed down my cheek as I jolted from my chair and paced around the office. What in the world was happening? Some sort of scorching lemon/acid concoction had undeniably squeezed its way inside my eyelid.

What I didn't realize, but was painfully learning, was this: I had smeared the menthol rub over my entire face and later dragged a generous blob of it onto my eyeball. I couldn't see the transparent ointment at the time, but later I definitely felt its' painful effects.

Girlfriend, have you ever been there? While it's not likely you've smeared salve unknowingly over your whole face but noticed your folly later, with teary eyes and in the company of umpteen witnesses, perhaps you've made poor decisions that were unnoticeable at the time but later led to agonizing results.

When I've found myself in this situation, I've had to come to a screeching halt, reflect, backtrack, and try to figure out how I got there. Unfortunately, many times my decisions have involved others and required confession, forgiveness, and grace. And through this there is growth—painful, stinging growth.

Girlfriend, we have this assurance,

"And I am sure of this, that he who began a good work in you will bring it to completion at the day of Jesus Christ" (Phil. 1:6).

Listen, Sister: I want to be more like Jesus, but I'm not terribly excited about this process. Thankfully God has His own agenda and loves me too much to leave me the way I am. I'm too chicken to ask Him to "grow me" because I know how painful growth is. And I'm not a big fan of pain—or Vicks in my eyes.

Choosing Joy in the Journey

L et me take you back again to our freakshow era, a time when our home was bursting at the seams with whiny toddlers, energetic children, and moody teenagers sporting raging hormones. Groceries vanished before our very eyes, and we kept a pair of Holstein busy supplying the milk necessary to sustain our tribe.

We encouraged summer jobs, and Jesse's started bright and early and a few miles away from home. He needed a ride.

Early morning didn't mean the house was peaceful, enveloped in dark solitude. No, our family included a couple of early rising tykes looking to fill their bellies. "Mom, Mama, Mommy, Mom" filled the air the moment their eyes popped open. Darlings. Rest for me was light years away.

I remember the chaotic swirl of morning activity, throwing together some sort of PB&C (peanut butter & cheese whiz) delight and leaving "the littles" in the care of a responsible sibling as I escaped the ruckus to taxi our son. Be right back.

Now, I don't know about you, but to this day my last "minute" of walking out the door is rarely only a minute long. Predictably, I grab one more forgotten item, turn off an appliance, flip a light switch, leave further instructions, sign a note, pull meat out of the freezer for dinner, and break up a fight while pulling the door closed behind me.

With pleasure, I pulled onto the road, proudly glancing over at my industrious son and down at the dash of my trusty station wagon. It was then I first noticed the needle leaning hard on *E*.

Duh!

Lord, please let us get to town. Please don't let my boy be late for work. Also, if he didn't hate me, that would be good.

In my mind's eye, I flipped through the possible scenarios:

- Deliver my son to work safely and on time (my preferred choice).
- Trot down the edge of the road in painful silence beside a sulking teenager as I accept full responsibility for the empty tank.
- Stand on the shoulder of 21 Highway with my thumb out, begging goodness knows who to pick us up and (hopefully) deliver us to the next town.

Right around that time, it occurred to me that I was still wearing my pajamas. Friend, this was years before it was in any way common or acceptable to wear pajamas in public. There wasn't a Walmart within one hundred miles of here. And these pjs were not your standard "hanging out at home" comfy flannel pants. Nope. Picture an ill-fitting, threadbare mishmash of short shorts and my husband's old T-shirt that begged to be thrown out years before. Lord, have mercy.

The impending humiliation burned within my chest. Beads of sweat lined my forehead, and I prayed even more earnestly for the car to stay in motion.

As I dropped Jesse off at work and continued to the gas station, I exhaled a deep sigh of relief. I made it. Relaxing safely out of sight as the attendant filled my car with gas, I watched the early morning rush of customers streaming in and out. Commuters fueled up, and locals grabbed a coffee, complaining about the bean crops.

And then it happened. The gas boy approached my window to deliver the bad news. The computer in the kiosk was not working; I would need to proceed inside to pay. I had almost made it.

And in I went, in all my glory: morning face, messy hair, ugly pajamas, and thankful heart. Whatever the circumstance, whatever the outcome, let's be determined to find something to be thankful for:

"Rejoice always, pray continually, give thanks in all circumstances; for this is God's will for you in Christ Jesus" (1 Thess. 5:16–18).

I choose joy. I could have chosen to be upset and embarrassed. Or I could be thankful that I wasn't forced to hitch a ride. Because believe me, chances are, nobody was stopping to pick me up that day.

Listen, Sister: Today I want to embrace thankfulness. It's our choice to make, isn't it? I bet you've been involved in a few unexpected situations, too. Find something today to be thankful for.

A Grand Adventure

Last summer I embarked on a crazy-lady-next-door sort of adventure, without intending to. Now that I think about it, I doubt I've ever tried to get involved in these kinds of things. It just happens.

It all started when I learned that the rice-sized black specks on my parsley plant were actually teeny, tiny baby caterpillars with incredibly huge appetites. Daily I watched as they quickly grew to be vibrant, lime-green monsters, chomping away all day, oblivious to my special interest.

After some research, I learned that a caterpillar doesn't leave his food source his entire larva life. So, in a bold move, I brought the plants inside and set them up in the front windowsill. I gave my new friends sunshine and all the food they could eat, safely tucked away from the threat of any hungry predator looking for a juicy meal. We named them Bob and Doug because, well, we're Canadian, eh?

I'd highly recommend caterpillars as pets as they are very low maintenance with no litter box or poop scooping to be done. Plus, they are incredibly interesting to watch.

Eventually, out of nowhere, the day we knew would happen did. Bob set out on a grand adventure made known only to him by his Creator. I won't tell you exactly where his day-long escapade took him, but suffice it to say, it included some precarious locations and covered a remarkable amount of ground, considering how slowly he moseyed along.

After hours of distracting us with his shenanigans, Bob crawled up a make-shift tripod of sticks and then just stopped, curled up, and went to sleep.

As expected, within a few short hours, my vibrant, beautiful caterpillar transformed into an ugly, dreadful, comatose-grey lump. I was heartbroken. Although I knew it would happen, it was still a dismal sight to see.

Days turned into weeks, and the cocoon hung dark, seemingly life-less, until late one afternoon. Checking in, I was shocked to see it deserted. Perched inches below, drying his wings, I spotted the most exquisite butter-fly I had ever seen.

But let's recap, Friends: Before this beauty came the ugly, the seemingly dead. The struggle gave way to incredible beauty. And things were not at all as they had seemed.

This whole scene reminded me of my dad. Big, hot tears slide down my face as I remember that not long ago, cancer wreaked havoc on his poor body. He endured much pain and suffering. But listen, my dad didn't stay there. *That was not the end of the story.* And that's why we have hope, Sister.

I know that I will see my dad again. I know that he will have a new body, one that's perfect. This is truth. This is why I have hope, and you can too:

"Therefore we do not lose heart. Though outwardly we are wasting away, yet inwardly we are being renewed day by day. For our light and momentary troubles are achieving for us an eternal glory that far outweighs them all. So we fix our eyes not on what is seen, but on what is unseen, since what is seen is temporary, but what is unseen is eternal" (2 Cor. 4:16–18).

Listen, Sister: How about you? Are you struggling in a dark time? It's true. There is sadness and loss, but we have hope in Christ. He Himself conquered death so that we don't have to stay there. Ask Him for help today.

Out of Place

Years ago, Ricky and I took the rare opportunity to catch a show at the local theatre. I say rare because our eighth son was less than a year old, and we had neither the time nor the funds for such extravagance. Looking back, I have no idea how we pulled it off. Maybe we didn't buy ketchup. Our monthly ketchup budget was roughly the cost of two movie tickets, not including popcorn.

He chose *Starsky and Hutch* because of our mutual admiration for the '70s television show. And who doesn't thrill to the sounds of undercover cops, car chases, drug lords, and disco music? All the feels, right there.

The movie itself was a huge disappointment. The characters were lame, the storyline hard to follow, and not once did anyone slide across the hood of a Grand Torino. A total bomb.

Making our way to the lobby, I spotted a couple we had recently met at church. We were relatively new to the "church thing," and I was eager to make friends and fit in. Taking full advantage of the opportunity to commiserate on the disappointing film, we rushed over.

Surprisingly, the conversation went something like this:

Them: "Oh, hi! Wasn't that sooo good?"

Me: Pausing awkwardly, I wondered if I was discerning sarcasm in my new friend.

Them: "I mean, I just couldn't bear it."

Me: Still not responding, I was cautious. Although I also couldn't bear it, I felt the overwhelming sense that we were not on the same page here.

Them: "Especially the ending; there wasn't a dry eye in the house."

Confused, I glanced up and noticed the lobby chock-full of Christians. I could tell they were Christians because of the hometown reunion atmosphere and the hugging. They were chatting, wiping tears, and clearly moved within.

And then it dawned on me. Actually, Ricky and I both caught on simultaneously. Everyone else, the lobby full of people, had just experienced *The Passion of the Christ*, which was in no way, shape, or form *Starsky and Hutch*.

We skedaddled out of there quickly, somehow feeling inadequate, like we didn't fit in. To be clear, not one person made me feel this way. It was just me. Also, I did not offer up the fact that we had actually watched a totally different show or correct any assumptions made by the good people.

Coming back to church, and to God really, was an arduous journey. Years of rebellion and horrible decisions—and the resulting consequences—weighed heavily on my heart. I shouldered a great deal of shame and guilt, wearing it like a prickly wool turtleneck knitted by Nana. It was heavy and restricting, yet I felt unworthy to remove it.

There were people who remembered my past and were not keen on welcoming me back into the fold, but the people of Bluewater were lovely. Hear me when I tell you, the struggle was inside my own head.

The enemy tormented me, reminding me continually of my history, my struggles, and my failures. *Why even bother? I can never be like "them." I can never measure up. If they only knew.*

Have you ever felt this way? Like you couldn't measure up and were not good enough for people, certainly not good enough for God?

The enemy may feed us lies about our identity, ushering shame and regret into our thoughts. But the truth is, once we accept God's gift of salvation, we are forever His. And even if we look different on the outside or choose different movie genres, we are forever part of the clan, forever His children:

> "See what great love the Father has lavished on us, that we should be called children of God! And that is what we are!" (1 John 3:1).

Listen, Sister: Only Jesus led a perfect life, and then He sacrificed it for you and me to pay the price for our sin. He set me free from my past, free from the requirement to somehow measure up. He wipes us clean, rescues us from sin, and welcomes us into his family.

Big-Family Hacks

Although my husband often refers to our huge family as "the freak-show," it was only recently that I learned the true sense of the word. I've since veered away from a near catastrophe, almost using it as a hashtag. (Don't do it.) Our freakshow was more of a "wow, this life is really nuts" sort of situation.

From treacherous elastic wars to the never-ending spontaneous wrestling matches on the kitchen floor, our home was a hive of chaotic activity every single day. And, Girlfriend, parents were outnumbered four to one.

Raising a considerable brood obviously differs from navigating life in a family of a more reasonable size. Cruise vacations and trips to the Bahamas were not in the books for us, but we did manage to make loads of memories along the way, and some were even positive.

Although I am indeed a girl, the creative, decorative, fancy side of my brain is essentially inoperable. As such, I find cooking for a crowd easier than preparing a beautiful dinner for two. I can make chili for a hundred, but it won't look pretty. The childhood meals I prepared back in the day may not have been aesthetically pleasing, but the boys ate and grew, and, hey, I'm calling that a win. Every kid was allowed one food they could graciously bow out of eating, opting to make their own peanut butter sandwich instead. This list was posted on the refrigerator and agreed upon, like all sane families do, I suppose. Because Sister, I was *not* a walking buffet for eight kids to pick from.

Along the way, there were bumps on the parenting road, of course. Some were little speed bumps, which we wore down in no time. Others jammed us up for longer. One such annoyance was the ever-present pile of shoes constantly sprawled out just inside the front door.

Every day, my husband would come home from work, open the door, and lose his footing, stumbling headlong into the hallway surrounded by a mountain of sneakers of various shapes and sizes. The scene was reminiscent of the opening credits of the old *Dick Van Dyke Show*, only with more cussing. After numerous attempts to "encourage" the boys to store their shoes off to the side or (crazy thought) put them away, we formulated a plan. We took any wayward pairs of shoes and tied the laces together tightly, chucking them out the front door. This passive-aggressive approach at parenting gave the children a few extra minutes to consider their actions while sitting on the sidewalk untangling their knotted laces. It wasn't a perfect plan, but I recommend it just the same.

We always ate dinner together, a table full of people I loved. It was the best. Not to brag, but we were once on a roll of over twenty days in a row of spilled milk before that record ended. Good times.

There were sad days too. Every so often, a bay leaf or a wayward chicken bone was spotted in a bowl of soup. The world as we knew it nearly came to an end until we instilled the "lucky leaf" strategy where anything different and not desired automatically became lucky. Lucky bone, lucky leaf, lucky chipped plate—you get the idea. It was brilliant.

As in any family of boys, we were all competitive, of course, and board games were the most common form of entertainment. When the middle five were teens, we held the record for playing Settlers every single day for over a year, always fighting for the honour of High Lord or High Lady of Catan. All these years later, this is still a thing at our house, and you are cordially invited to take up the challenge.

Always the fun guy, Ricky was a wiz at using our common, everyday items to generate lasting memories with the boys. These were his specialties:

- Apple Baseball: This is the self-explanatory sport of smashing over-ripe and undesirable fruit with a bat across the field, competing for distance and showmanship.
- Chuck the Pumpkin: Popular in early November, this is a competition where no longer useful jack-o'-lanterns were flung over the upper balcony rail, contending for best pumpkin splatter-ability.

Parenting this big band of brothers, we learned fun doesn't have to be fancy, and while days may be long, years are short. I look back and see the blessing in raising these young men:

"Like arrows in the hands of a warrior are children born in one's youth. Blessed is the man whose quiver is full of them. They will not be put to shame when they contend with their opponents in court" (Ps. 127:4–5).

Listen, Sister: I do miss the fun, the games, and the laughter around the table—not so much the spilled milk. What are some of your fun memories? Consider journaling to record these stories.

About the Author

Tess Scott, former black sheep turned Jesus Girl, is the proud mom of eight boys and spunky Grami (with a heart above the *i*) to a whole slew of adorable grandkids. She began the Listen, Sister! Encouragement for Women ministry in 2020. You can find her blog posts at www.listensister.ca and her Listen, Sister! Encouragement for Women pages on Facebook and Instagram. She continues to live her life of hilariously awkward moments in Sarnia, Ontario, to the ongoing embarrassment of her family.

Tess would love to hear from you: e-mail her at tess@listensister.ca. She is also eager to bring her freakshow story to your event to inspire and encourage women. Check out listensister.ca for details.

A free ebook edition is available with the purchase of this book.

To claim your free ebook edition:

1. Visit MorganJamesBOGO.com
2. Sign your name CLEARLY in the space
3. Complete the form and submit a photo of the entire copyright page
4. You or your friend can download the ebook to your preferred device

A FREE ebook edition is available for you or a friend with the purchase of this print book.

CLEARLY SIGN YOUR NAME ABOVE

Instructions to claim your free ebook edition:
1. Visit MorganJamesBOGO.com
2. Sign your name CLEARLY in the space above
3. Complete the form and submit a photo of this entire page
4. You or your friend can download the ebook to your preferred device

Print & Digital Together Forever.

Snap a photo

Free ebook

Read anywhere